Searching fo
The U.S. Development of Constabulary Forces in Latin America and the Philippines

Dr. Richard L. Millett

Occasional Paper 30

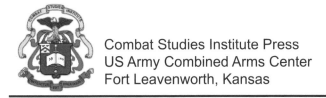

Combat Studies Institute Press
US Army Combined Arms Center
Fort Leavenworth, Kansas

Library of Congress Cataloging-in-Publication Data

Millett, Richard, 1938-
  Searching for stability : the U.S. development of constabulary forces in Latin America and the Philippines / Richard L. Millett.
    p. cm. -- (Occasional paper / Combat Studies Institute ; 30)
  Includes bibliographical references.
  1. Police training--Caribbean Area--History--20th century. 2. Police training--Philippines--History--20th century. 3. Police--Philippines--History--20th century. 4. Police--Caribbean Area--History--20th century. 5. Military assistance, American--Caribbean Area--History--20th century. 6. Military assistance, American--Philippines--History--20th century. 7. United States. Armed Forces--Stability operations--History--20th century. I. Title. II. Series.

  HV8170.A2M557 2010
  363.209729--dc22

                                        2010007718

Foreword

The Combat Studies Institute is pleased to present Occasional Paper 30, *Searching for Stability: The US Development of Constabulary Forces in Latin America and the Philippines,* by Dr. Richard L. Millett. In this study, Dr. Millett offers a survey of U.S. military involvement in the training of indigenous security forces in the Philippines and the Caribbean Basin in the 20th century. Given the dramatic increase of these types of efforts in Iraq, Afghanistan, and other countries, this study provides relevant insights for current military professionals facing the daunting challenges that are inherent to the training and advising of foreign police and military forces.

Dr. Millett's succinct analysis highlights several critical themes common to the American experience in these types of missions. First and foremost, despite all the best attempts to involve other departments of the federal government, the U.S. military has historically served as the lead, and often the sole, U.S. agency in these efforts. This fact often translated into constabulary training programs that suffered from a lack of both guidance and resources. Put simply, the relatively few Soldiers and Marines working on these efforts - many of whom were relatively junior in rank - were forced to make important military and political decisions that had critical effects on the host nation as well as on U.S. foreign policy. Additionally, this study emphasizes the traditional strains between U.S. goals and host nation desires, tensions that were often exacerbated by U.S. personnel who knew little or nothing about the culture in which they were working and had no ability to speak the language of those they were training. Dr. Millett suggests that these problems contributed to the important but flawed assumption among both U.S. policymakers and American military officers that indigenous forces trained by the U.S. military would behave like the U.S. military. Unfortunately, rather than becoming the professional security forces that served stable representative governments, these constabularies often became tools of unsteady repressive regimes.

Given the geopolitical challenges facing the United States in the early 21st Century and the Department of Defense's focus on creating a military that can conduct stability operations in a variety of countries, the mission to train and advise foreign security forces is unlikely to disappear any time soon. This study offers an important set of insights from the past that can contribute to a sharper understanding about the challenges of building and advising these forces in the future. CSI – The Past Is Prologue!

Dr. William G. Robertson
Director, Combat Studies Institute

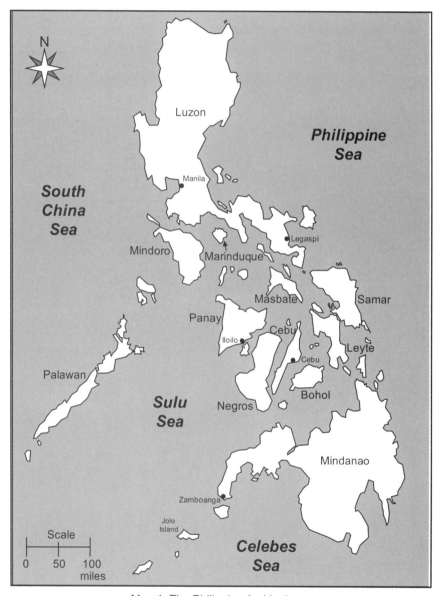

Map 1. The Philippine Archipelago.

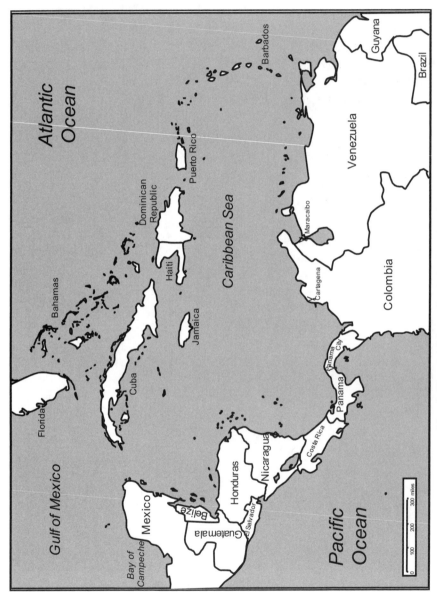

Map 2. The Caribbean Basin in the 20th Century.

Contents

Chapter 1

Introduction

There is remarkably little literature available on American efforts to create and train security forces in other nations. Only a few studies focusing on specific cases are available, many published by the US Army. The topic is included but rarely emphasized in studies of American interventions. There is no broad-based study examining the American experience in several different nations and no literature, at least in English, comparing the American military experience with that of other nations such as the United Kingdom, France, or the Soviet Union. Hopefully, this volume will begin to fill in some of these gaps and will inspire others to examine the prospects and pitfalls of such projects and the limits of influence that constrain all such efforts.

Prior to 1898, the United States had little experience in creating military or police forces in other nations. In addition, we had virtually no experience with constabulary-type forces of our own, in part because *posse comitatus* seemed to forbid this combination of military and internal police functions. The closest parallel may have been the creation of various units among the Native Americans such as Apache Scouts and Reservation Police. In the last third of the nineteenth century, Reservation Police were a major project of the Bureau of Indian Affairs, in part because of pressures to replace the military in policing reservations. The squads received very little training from the Army or from anyone else.[1]

The Spanish–American War of 1898 and the decision to construct a canal through Panama a few years later dramatically changed the American interest in creating and training constabularies. The United States found itself responsible for internal security in the Philippines and Cuba and for maintaining security in the new nation of Panama. In short order, Haiti, the Dominican Republic, and Nicaragua became virtual protectorates of the United States. Chronic instability in Central America and on the island of Hispaniola (shared by Haiti and the Dominican Republic) had previously been of little concern in Washington, DC, but the proliferation of American territories and bases in the region combined with the opening of the Panama Canal suddenly made stability in this region a major policy concern.[2]

For a variety of reasons the United States found it difficult to acknowledge that it had become a colonial power. As a result, no Colonial Office or service was ever created, no body of civilian specialists put together to manage these new responsibilities. This even applied to the establishment of Customs Receiverships in various nations. Responsibility was given to the War and Navy Departments who administered most of the territories as well as running operations in the protectorates. War Department responsibilities were centered in the Bureau of Insular Affairs which was created in 1898 and, at one point or another, had administrative jurisdiction over Puerto Rico, the Philippines, the first and second military governments in Cuba, and Customs Receiverships in Haiti and the Dominican Republic.[3] The Navy ran the Virgin Islands until 1931, Guam until 1950, and American Samoa until 1951. Government in the Canal Zone was a matter of prolonged controversy, but for most of its existence the Governor was an active-duty Army officer.[4]

Shortly after the Spanish–American War another development impacted American operations in the new territories and protectorates. That was the rapid development of wireless radio. This gave Washington the opportunity to exercise much closer supervision over operations in the field and also gave newspapers and other media increased opportunities to report on developments. The independent authority of those operating in the field was reduced and the potential for friction between those who made policies and those charged with their enactment increased.

Adapting US policies to this changed environment proved difficult and controversial. One reflection of this was the creation of the "Roosevelt Corollary" to the Monroe Doctrine, included in President Theodore Roosevelt's 1905 State of the Union Message. Roosevelt declared:

> It is always possible that wrong actions toward this Nation or toward citizens of this nation, in some State unable to keep order among its own people, unable to secure justice for outsiders, and unwilling to do justice to those outsiders who treat it well, may result in our having to take action to protect our rights; but such action will not be taken with a view to territorial aggression, and it will be taken if at all only with extreme reluctance and when it has become evident that every other resource has been exhausted.[5]

While never legally binding, the Corollary would be cited and expanded by subsequent administrations. In November 1915, Woodrow Wilson's Secretary of State, Robert Lansing, wrote:

> The United States should expand the application of the Monroe Doctrine and declare as a definite Caribbean policy that, while it does not seek domination over the territory of any of these republics, it is necessary for the na-

tional safety of the United States, and particularly in view of its interests on the isthmus of Panama, that it aid the people of those republics in establishing and maintaining honest and responsible governments to such extent as may be necessary in each particular case.[6]

This justification for interventions, past and present, brought the United States directly into what would much later be described as "nation building." The development of security forces would be a vital part of this mission. Dr. Dana Gardner Munro, who held several key State Department posts in Central America and the Caribbean during the 1920s and 30s, recalled:

The establishment of nonpartisan constabularies in the Caribbean states was one of the chief objectives of our policy from the time it became clear that the customs collectorships wouldn't assure stability by themselves. The old armies were or seemed to be one of the principal causes of disorder and financial disorganization. They consumed most of the government's revenue, chiefly in graft, and they gave nothing but disorder and oppression in return. We thought that a disciplined force, trained by Americans, would do away with the petty local oppression that was responsible for much of the disorder that occurred and would be an important step toward better financial administration and economic progress generally.[7]

Other aspects of these nation-building efforts would include government reorganization, election supervision, road building, improved health and sanitation, and judicial reform. In most of these projects the newly created security forces became involved. Once American tutelage ended these forces usually proved reluctant to give up their expanded roles. The combination of military and police functions in a single body also made the new constabularies a potentially powerful political force in their own right.

Beginning in 1899 in the Philippines, the American assumption of responsibility for internal security brought the United States into direct involvement in prolonged civil conflicts, first there and later in Haiti, the Dominican Republic, and Nicaragua. In each case the desire to reduce American casualties and extricate forces made the creation of native troops an increasingly urgent priority.[8] In the process, the original emphasis on using these forces for policing functions was reduced and increased emphasis given to military capabilities. In every case, Americans, usually military on active duty, not only undertook training, but filled some, if not all, of the positions as officers in the field. The military was now involved in policing, sanitation, internal communications, and sometimes even in exercising judicial authority over civilian populations. All this was done with severely constrained resources, little doctrinal preparation or guidance, limited if not nonexistent language skills, and in the context of prevailing racial, cultural, and religious prejudices. The task proved to be a formidable one.

Relations with domestic political forces varied widely over time and place. There was rarely any genuine interest in the creation of a professional, nonpartisan force that would not serve largely the interests of whatever faction was in power. There were also issues of national sovereignty and not wanting to cede control over the forces responsible for maintaining order and defending sovereignty to a foreign power. At the same time, those in power were not unhappy to have a more powerful and capable force with which to confront revolutionary outbreaks. Central governments also saw such forces as a means of breaking the power of regional strongmen.

Events in the wider world impinged on these efforts. Resources in the Philippines were strained by the diversion of troops to China during the Boxer Rebellion and later by the coming of war with Japan. World War I had a major impact, especially in Haiti and the Dominican Republic, draining men and supplies, diverting the attention of Washington, and creating a new dimension of internal security concerns where there was a significant German presence. Japanese attacks in Manchuria caused Secretary of State Henry Stimson to accelerate the pace of American withdrawal from Haiti and Nicaragua so as to strengthen the moral case for opposition to Japanese intervention. The Great Depression also made Washington anxious to cut costs and conserve the resources connected with the interventions.

Finally, domestic politics were frequently a disruptive factor. Changes in administrations brought changes in policy objectives and methods. Congressional investigations, especially in the Philippines and Haiti, both diverted attention and forced operational changes. A vocal minority in both Congress and the press kept up a barrage of criticism and negative publicity. Intervention policies were an issue in several elections, most notably in 1912 and 1920. Political decisions led to turnover of newly created forces to national command much sooner than many in the military thought wise or prudent.

Under these circumstances, what is perhaps surprising is not the array of problems that confronted efforts to develop these forces, but the surprising degree of at least short-term success of most of these efforts. Relative peace, if not democratic government, was restored, transfers to national authorities completed, and in the short run, US influence, if not control,

4

largely maintained. Longer-range results would be much less favorable, but this was something those charged with creating the new security forces could neither envision nor control. The basic question in every case was the same: would the price of the stability achieved ultimately prove too high?

Notes

1. For details on the training of Reservation Police, see Michael Lynn Barker, "American Indian Tribal Police: An Overview and a Case Study" (Ph.D. dissertation, State University of New York–Albany, 1994), 44–60. Remarkably little has been published on this subject.

2. The United States established military bases in Puerto Rico, at both ends of the Canal Zone in Panama, at Guantanamo Bay in Cuba, and in the Virgin Islands. In addition, interest was occasionally expressed in acquiring additional bases in Hispaniola and in the Gulf of Fonseca between Nicaragua and Honduras.

3. Records of the Bureau of Insular Affairs, RG 350, 1868–1945, http:// www.archives.gov/research/guide-fed-record groups/350.html. For a history of the War Department's Bureau of Insular Affairs, see Earl S. Pomeroy, "America's Colonial Office," *The Mississippi Valley Historical Review,* Vol. 30 (March 1944), 521–532.

4. For details on this see John Major, *Prize Possession: The United States and the Panama Canal, 1903–1979* (Cambridge, UK: Cambridge University Press, 1993), 69–77.

5. Text included in Dexter Perkins, *A History of the Monroe Doctrine* (Revised edition) (Boston, MA: Little Brown & Co., 1955), 228–229. Perkins goes on to discuss how this Corollary led to repeated interventions.

6. "Memorandum by Secretary of State Robert Lansing for President Woodrow Wilson, November 24, 1915," *Papers Relating to the Foreign Affairs of the United States: The Lansing Papers*, Vol. II (Washington, DC: Government Printing Office, 1940), 466.

7. Letter from Dr. Dana Gardner Munro to author, 14 February 1965.

8. For details on these conflicts, see Lester Langley, *The Banana Wars: An Inner History of American Empire, 1900–1934* (Lexington, KY: The University Press of Kentucky, 1983); Max Boot, *The Savage Wars of Peace: Small Wars and the Rise of American Power* (New York, NY: Basic Books, 2002).

Chapter 2

The Philippines: Becoming a Colonial Power

The Philippines were America's first, and perhaps most successful experience, in organizing foreign constabulary forces. The key was the total control the United States, as the ruling colonial power, had over the islands and the expectation that such control would continue for an indefinite period. These conditions would not be replicated in later experiences in the Caribbean, but American officials repeatedly cited the Philippine experience as both a justification of and a model for these later efforts and as an example of a successful counterinsurgency. Officers with experience in the Philippines were frequently called on for service in subsequent constabulary-creating efforts, most notably in Nicaragua in 1924. This makes the history of the Philippine Constabulary both relevant and informative when evaluating subsequent efforts.

The American takeover of the Philippines from Spain had proved surprisingly easy. Gaining effective control over this vast archipelago, however, would prove much more difficult. At first Washington seemed unsure about what to do with this territory. President McKinley told a group of Methodists that he was compelled to seek divine guidance as to what course to pursue. After fervent prayer he determined that America had an obligation "to educate the Filipinos and uplift and Christianize them."[1] He hoped that this could be done peacefully and that the Filipinos would come to understand that we had their good interests at heart. This hope was to prove tragically misplaced.

Besides the newly arrived American forces and the remnants of Spanish colonial units, there were two other armed groups active in the Philippines. One was armed Muslims in the south, notably on Samar and Mindanao. More numerous and better organized and armed was a revolutionary army led by Emilio Aguinaldo. He had already begun organizing a government and had large forces near Manila. His initial hopes that the Americans would support an independent government were soon dashed and tensions steadily increased.[2] Fighting broke out in early 1899 and the resultant conflict was prolonged and costly. Over 122,000 American military personnel were ultimately sent to the Philippines, although average monthly strength for the two and a half years of official combat averaged only forty thousand. More American troops were killed in action in putting down what was termed the Philippine Insurrection than were lost in the Spanish–American War.[3]

On 4 July 1902, President Theodore Roosevelt proclaimed the Insurrection at an end, but fighting continued, especially against the Muslim insurgents known as Moros, for several more years.[4] Indeed the last organized Moro resistance did not end until 1916. The fighting strained the Army's resources, generated considerable controversy at home, and produced numerous accounts of alleged Army atrocities.[5] An additional complicating factor was the need to dispatch American troops from the Philippines to China to help put down the Boxer Rebellion. General Arthur MacArthur, the Army's commander in the Philippines, constantly resisted Washington's demands that he dispatch units, complaining that, as a result, his forces had "been decimated to limit of safety."[6]

The Army was also reluctant to take on policing duties throughout the Islands. Under the Spanish these had largely been left to the *Guardia Civil*, which, according to one source, was "regarded with detestation and terror by the people."[7] A municipal police, under close American control, was soon organized for Manila, but the rest of the country had little in the way of law enforcement. Further complicating the issue was the domination of most courts by local elites and the multitude of languages and dialects spoken throughout the archipelago.

All of these factors combined to make it imperative to raise native forces to assist in and eventually take over both the fighting and basic police duties. Taking advantage of local feuds, the Americans had quickly recruited groups of local auxiliaries, some of whom proved quite effective. But, stronger, more disciplined forces were needed. Ultimately, the decision was reached to create two separate units, one of which would be incorporated within the American military structure, while the other would be a national militarized police force. These would become the Philippine Scouts and the Philippine Constabulary.

The Scouts began on 10 September 1899 with the recruitment of 100 soldiers, from the minority Macabebes. Commanded by First Lieutenant Matthew Betson of the US Army, they performed so well that four more companies were formed in October. Other minority populations were later recruited, but for years there were no units from the majority Tagalog population due to American distrust and fears of their ties to the insurgents.[8] Reliance on the Scouts increased constantly and, by June 1901, there were 5,400 of them serving with the American Army.[9]

Ultimately, the Scouts became part of the American Army, forming the heart of the "Philippine Division." Their budget was provided by the United States, but enlisted men drew a significantly smaller pay than their American counterparts. At first, all officers were American, but slowly Filipinos took over the field grade officer positions. Higher posts remained in American hands. In one important aspect the Scouts, and later the Constabulary, differed from European colonial armies. They were specifically prohibited from serving outside the Philippines.

As time passed, combat increasingly was taken over by Scout units, especially on Samar. In 1904, at the start of the fighting, there were twelve American Army companies and six Scout companies there. Three years later, there were eighteen Scout companies and only two American.[10] The growing reliance on the Scouts had the additional advantage of reducing American casualties and, consequently, some of the criticism of our occupation of the Islands.

The Scouts role in combat left the task of policing the countryside still unfilled. Expanding the Scouts would have also expanded the cost to the US budget, something that Washington wanted to avoid. However, some Army officers argued for Scout expansion, not wanting to see any armed force in the Islands outside of their control. In addition, the Army had undertaken the informal recruiting of local auxiliaries, often taking advantage of local ethnic and religious rivalries. While justified as a necessity at the height of combat these "unsavory allies" all too often were "motivated by revenge, tribal vendettas, or just bad character."[11] Another force was needed to undertake policing duties, and maintain control in rural areas while coming under closer American control. Governor William Howard Taft decided that the civil, not the military authority must control such a force and on 1 August 1901 the Philippine Commission issued Act 175 which created an independent Philippine Constabulary.[12] In October, in a report to the Secretary of War, the Philippine Commission outlined their plan:

> To create an insular force of not exceeding one hundred and fifty men for each province, selected from the natives thereof, who may be mounted in whole or part, and who are placed under the command of one or more, not exceeding four, provincial inspectors. The whole body is placed under the control of a chief and four assistant chiefs of constabulary. . . . Full powers are given to properly arm, equip, maintain and discipline the force, which is enlisted for two years, unless sooner discharged. They are declared to be peace officers and it is their special duty to prevent and suppress brigandage, insurrection, unlawful assemblies, and breaches of the peace. For this purpose they are given authority to make arrests, but are

required at the earliest possible moment to bring the prisoner before a magistrate for examination.[13]

Providing officers was an immediate issue. The Army detailed only a few active duty officers to fill the most senior posts. The rest were drawn from a variety of sources. Some were American volunteers who had mustered out in the Philippines, others were regular Army non-commissioned officers who had been discharged, and a small number were Filipinos.[14] These were a mixed lot. Some were drunks or had other character defects.[15] Almost all the Americans were former enlisted men who had no experience and were evidently given little training as officers. Enlisted personnel also came from various backgrounds, including some former members of the hated *Guardia Civil*. Despite budget limitations and the problems of finding suitable recruits, the force grew quickly, reaching over 2,000 men by early 1902.

The Constabulary had a rocky beginning. They confronted the remnants of Aguinaldo's revolutionary forces, fanatical Islamic insurgents, and organized banditry. While their opponents were well armed the Constabulary was at first given only light weapons, notably single shot Remington shotguns. This was in part because critics in the Army and in the civilian government feared they might desert, taking their weapons with them.[16] Ultimately, this prejudice was overcome and more modern arms supplied, but only after some disastrous engagements.

Poorly armed, ill-trained, and, at times, not well led, the new force attracted considerable criticism. One American critic, who served as a judge in the Philippines, charged that the Constabulary was "wholly inadequate . . . for the maintenance of public order," and, as a result, "by 1903 brigandage therein was thriving like a garden of weeds."[17] Philippine Commission member Dean C. Worcester explained this: "The organization of a rural police force was imperatively necessary. Unfortunately, the most critical situation which it would be call upon to meet had to be faced at the very outset when both officers and men were inexperienced and before adequate discipline could be established."[18] At first called the Insular Constabulary the title was soon changed to Philippine Constabulary. An intelligence unit, known as the Secret Service, was established within the force and eventually became the major source of information not only on insurgents and criminals, but also on foreign citizens living in the islands. By 1909, they were furnishing the War Department a forty-three page summary of Japanese activities.[19]

There was significant early friction between the Constabulary and the Scouts, especially when they served near each other in conflicted areas. The Scouts looked down on the Constabulary as a markedly inferior force, while the Constabulary's commander constantly sought to expand his force's authority at the expense of the Scouts.[20] These disputes would continue on for several years. At the same time, it became increasingly common for Scout and Constabulary units to mount joint operations, most of which proved successful. During 1903, for example, there were 357 hostile contacts by Constabulary units that claimed to have killed 1,185 "outlaws," and captured another 2,722 men.[21] By 1911, when the last organized resistance ceased, the Constabulary claimed to have killed 4,862 and captured 11,977 men. Constabulary losses totaled 11 officers and 197 enlisted killed in action plus 48 officers and 991 men who died of disease.[22]

As time passed, the Constabulary's capacity and reputation slowly improved. More and more Filipinos became officers, with some rising to the rank of Captain. Instruction was provided for potential officers and non-commissioned officers, but virtually all of it was conducted in English that severely limited enrollment. The Army's appreciation of the Constabulary's contribution also rose. In part this may have been due to cost savings. A US Army enlisted man earned $1,400 a year, a member of the Constabulary only $363.50. In addition, Constabulary enlisted men drew only ten and a half cents a day for rations.[23] Of even greater importance, while almost all Scout expenses came out of the Army's budget, only the salaries of the top seven or eight Constabulary officers did.[24]

The Constabulary also relieved the Army and the Scouts of most police duty and took over the more isolated posts. Because they were largely recruited locally, they had a good knowledge of local terrain and political structures and could speak local languages. This gave them a great advantage not only as police, but also in counterinsurgency operations. As one American officer observed, "Catching Filipino outlaws with the Army is like catching a flea in a 20-acre field with a traction engine."[25] The Constabulary's reliance on local recruits and the consequent ties to local families gave them a great advantage over both US Army and Scout units in small, local engagements. When led by officers who knew how to take advantage of these traits they often proved highly efficient.[26]

As peace was slowly imposed, the Constabulary began to concentrate on its other duties. Principal among these were regular rural police functions. They also undertook training and supervision of existing municipal police forces.[27] On occasion they clashed with local politicians, especially in cases were corruption or other malfeasance in office was alleged. Getting such individuals convicted, especially in local courts, was always a major problem, but the Constabulary did have some success.[28] They were never able, however, to break the power of local *caciques* nor end the patterns of abuse and corruption that would long continue to dominate many rural areas.

As peace returned the Constabulary's responsibilities steadily expanded into additional areas. While the fighting raged they had taken over the Army's responsibility for the control and maintenance of telegraph and telephone lines. These were eventually given to the Bureau of Posts, but the Constabulary acquired other duties. Outside of the major cities they became the firemen as well as the police. They were involved in public health programs, administering vaccinations, teaching rudimentary sanitation, and, on occasion, providing limited medical care. They undertook the building and maintenance of rural roads, both to enhance security and economic development. When a natural disaster occurred, an all too frequent event in an archipelago subject to violent typhoons, volcanic eruptions, and earthquakes, they provided relief, prevented looting, and helped with reconstruction.[29] Their police duties included attempting to prevent smuggling (something which was almost a Philippine tradition) and dealing with rampant livestock theft.[30] Their efforts in the latter effort were more successful.

As time passed, more and more Filipinos assumed the officer posts of the Constabulary. With the US entrance into World War I made the detailing of officers to the Islands even less desirable the process was essentially completed. A native Filipino, Brigadier General Rafael Cramé, became the Constabulary's commander. He continued in that post until his death in 1927.[31] By then the Constabulary had grown to a total of 6,223 officers and men.[32]

The Constabulary continued to function as a national militarized police until the Japanese invasion in December 1941. Some Americans continued to question the loyalty of the Scouts and Constabulary, especially after a near mutiny of the Scouts, largely over pay and related issues, in 1924. Plans for the Islands defense included the contingency of Scout and Constabulary defection, but fortunately there was never any occasion to put these into action.[33]

By the late 1930s American policy in the Philippines was complicated by two divergent trends. One was preparation of the Islands for their promised Independence. In early 1933, Congress passed a bill over President Hoover's veto, promising independence within ten years.[34] The other factor was the growing fear of war with Japan. General Douglas MacArthur was made a Field Marshall in the embryonic Philippine Army and set about trying to prepare a defense. He planned to create a national army with

12

one regular and thirty reserve divisions, but Depression economics and widespread opposition forced him to sharply curtail this project. Finding officers to train his reserves was a major issue. He had hoped to use the Philippine Scouts for this, but that proved largely impossible. Some officers were detailed from the Constabulary, but most of these preferred police work to military training.[35]

Eventually, MacArthur decided to incorporate the Constabulary as a division to be mobilized in case of war. But they were never given any real training for combat, never participated in large scale maneuvers with other units, and were so scattered among the islands as to make effective mobilization virtually impossible. MacArthur's plan to repel any attack on the beaches further insured that the Constabulary would never function as a cohesive military unit. The ultimate result was predictable. Some Constabulary units did join up with the rest of MacArthur's forces and retreated into the Bataan Peninsula where, along with the rest of the Philippine Army, they were ultimately destroyed. The remaining units were included in the overall surrender signed by General Jonathan Wainwright on 6 May 1942.

Some of the Constabulary formed or joined guerrilla units and continued to resist the Japanese occupation, but the force, as a whole, ceased to exist from 1942 until early 1945. They were then recreated and merged with the Military Police Command. Placed first under the Ministry of the Interior, but soon transferred to the Defense Ministry, the restored Constabulary was considered as part of the Philippine Armed Forces. Their officers graduated from the same Military Academy as regular army officers and it was not uncommon for officers to spend part of their career with both forces.[36] They played a major role in the fight against the Huk insurgency in the 1950s and 60s. At the same time some of their policing and most of their auxiliary duties were reduced and a separate National Police was formed. In 1986, Constabulary Commander, Major General Fidel Ramos, was a pivotal figure in the uprising that ousted Ferdinand Marcos from the Presidency and restored democratic rule to the Philippines.[37] Five years later, the Constabulary was merged with the National Police, ending its history as a separate force.

The Constabulary had performed reasonably well throughout most of its career. Its reputation was further enhanced by its role in the fall of Marcos. One key was the relatively swift and smooth transition to a national officer corps. Another was the fact that, while it performed some military functions, principle responsibilities in this area always rested with other forces. Finally, its early years were shaped by an American colonial administration that had an indefinite mandate. Efforts to apply the principles of the Philippine Constabulary in other nations would encounter fundamentally different conditions.

Notes

1. Quoted in Stuart Creighton Miller, *Benevolent Assimilation: The American Conquest of the Philippines, 1899–1903* (New Haven, CT: Yale University Press, 1982), 24.

2. For a description of the situation see John Morgan Gates, *Schoolbooks and Krags: The United States Army in the Philippines, 1898–1902* (Westport, CT: Greenwood Press, 1973), 13–33.

3. Exact casualty figures vary somewhat depending on what is included in the "Insurrection." *The New York Times* reported in 1918 that 741 were killed and another 225 later dies of wounds while 2,701 died of disease. "Our Casualties in Other Wars," *The New York Times*, 1 January 1918, 44.

4. There are numerous excellent accounts of the fighting in the Philippines. See, for example, Brian M. Linn, *The Philippine War, 1899–1902* (Lawrence, KS: University of Kansas Press, 2000); Robert D. Ramsey III, *Savage Wars of Peace: Case Studies of Pacification in the Philippines, 1900–1902*, The Long War Series Occasional Paper 24 (Fort Leavenworth, KS: The Combat Studies Institute Press, 2008).

5. For details on the US Army and Moro resistance, see Miller, *Benevolent Assimilation*.

6. Arthur MacArthur to Adjutant General, received 16 June 1900, *Correspondence Relating to the War with Spain Including the Insurrection in the Philippines and the China Relief Expedition, May 15, 1898 to July 30, 1902*, Vol. I (Washington, DC: US Government Printing Office, 1903), 412.

7. Dean C. Worcester, *The Philippines: Past and Present*, Vol. I (Whitefish, MT: Kessinger Publishing Company, 2004), 378–379. Worcester had as much experience in the Philippines as any American, serving on the two initial presidential Commissions sent to recommend policies for the Islands' government, then remaining for years as a senior official in the US administration of the Philippines.

8. Arnaldo Dumindin, "Philippine-American War, 1899–1902," http://www.freewebs.com/philippineamericanwar/thewarrages1899.htm. This study, written in 2006, seems only available on the web.

9. Gates, 213.

10. Brian McAllister Linn, *Guardians of Empire: The U.S. Army and the Pacific, 1902–1940* (Chapel Hill, NC: University of North Carolina Press, 1997), 48.

11. Brian McAllister Linn, "The U.S. Army and Nation Building and Pacification in the Philippines," in *Armed Diplomacy: Two Centuries of American Campaigning* (Fort Leavenworth, KS: Combat Studies Institute Press, 2004), 87.

12. Lieutenant Colonel Richard W. Smith, "Philippine Constabulary," *Military Review* (May 1968), 74.

13. Quoted in W. Cameron Forbes, *The Philippine Islands* (Millwood, NY: Kraus Reprint Company, 1976), 105.

14. Worcester, Vol. I, 381; Linn, *Guardians of Empire*, 19.

15. Smith, 74.

16. Ibid.

17. James H. Blount, *The American Occupation of the Philippines, 1898-1912* (New York, NY: G.P. Putnam's Sons, 1913), 403–404.

18. Worcester, Vol. I, 380–381.

19. Linn, *Guardians of Empire*, 107.

20. Ibid., 19.

21. Smith, 77.

22. Worcester, Vol. I, 398.

23. Ibid., 386–387.

24. Forbes, 118.

25. Quoted in Worcester, Vol. I, 385.

26. For one officer's account of duty with the Constabulary, see John R. White, *Bullets and Bolos: Fifteen Years in the Philippine Islands Fighting Insurgents with the Philippine Constabulary* (New York, NY: The Century Company, 1928).

27. Forbes, 108.

28. Smith, 79.

29. Worcester, Vol. I, 397–398.

30. Smith, 80.

31. Ramon J. Farolan, "Reveille: Anecdotes from the life of a constable," *Philippine Daily Inquirer*, 22 June 2009, http://opinion.inquirer.net/inquireropinion/columns/view/20090622-211740/Anecdotes-from-the-life-of-a-constable.

32. Forbes, 118.

33. Lind, *Guardians of Empire*, 148 and 158.

34. Stanley Karnow, *America's Empire in the Philippines* (New York, NY: Random House, 1989), 254.

35. Glen D. Gaddy, "MacArthur's Development of the Philippine Army and the Defense of the Islands, 1935–1942" (M.A. thesis, Southern Illinois University–Edwardsville, 1974), 55.

36. Farolan.

37. Karnow, 416–422.

Chapter 3

Cuba: Large Problems, Limited Influence

Like the Philippines, the US Army occupied Cuba as a result of the Spanish–American War. And, like the Philippines, Americans had to deal with a native revolutionary army that had been fighting the Spanish for several years. But there were major differences as well. While Filipinos spoke many different languages and were divided by religion, virtually all Cubans were Catholic and spoke Spanish. The bulk of the population was concentrated on a single island, and the terrain, while often difficult, was not nearly as inhospitable as much of the Philippines. There was a deep racial divide between those of European and those of African descent, but there was not the heritage of ethnic violence that characterized the Philippines.

The Philippines, like most of the territory acquired from Spain in 1898 was destined to remain under American rule for the foreseeable future. Cuba, however, was different. The United States had pledged to allow Cuba to become independent, but, at the same time, was determined to maintain a high degree of control. This made the transition from American military occupation to independence difficult and uncertain and insured that the formation and development of Cuban security forces would be a constant issue.

Occupied Cuba had two national forces in addition to the US military. There were remnants of the Spanish system, notably police, which had to be dealt with. One by one they were disarmed and the Spaniards later repatriated. But their absence left a law enforcement vacuum in many areas that the American occupying force was unwilling or unable to fill. As a result, some American authorities, starting with Colonel Leonard Wood in Santiago, began recruiting local forces, largely led by and composed of veterans of the Cuban Revolutionary Army.[1]

While a few members of the Revolutionary Army joined the embryonic police, many more remained with their units. They were a major force in internal politics as well as in military affairs. The outbreak of fighting in the Philippines left some American officers in Cuba fearful that similar events might occur there, but with Washington pledged to Cuban independence there was never any serious danger of conflict between the Americans and the revolutionaries. Dealing with them, however, presented problems. The American occupiers wanted them disarmed and disbanded as soon as possible, but had no clear plan as to what force, if any, might replace them. For most revolutionaries, their biggest concern was collecting the large amount of back pay they were owed. There were also concerns about future employment and, in some cases, a desire to use their military laurels as a springboard to national office.

Negotiations over disbanding this force were difficult and prolonged, but with the help of Cuba's senior general, Máximo Gómez, and three-million dollars from unexpended US War appropriations the bulk were ultimately disarmed with each soldier receiving $75.[2] There was some discontent over the relatively small amount received, but, in general, the process proceeded peacefully. Left unanswered was the question of what, if anything, would replace this force.

While most Cuban politicians wanted a national army, there were arguments against it, especially from the American point of view. Alone among the American republics, Cuba had no land frontiers with any other nation. This meant no boundary disputes, the major cause of Latin American wars, and no sanctuary in neighboring territory for rebel forces. The only credible external threat to Cuban sovereignty was that posed by the United States and the American Army obviously had no interest in helping Cuba defend itself against that. Finally, there was the omnipresent, if rarely mentioned, issue of race. A Cuban national army would include many Afro-Cubans, while the police forces the Americans were organizing were overwhelmingly white.[3] Virtually all American military officers at the start of the twentieth century rejected the idea of racially integrated units.

A military government was quickly established, with Major General John Brooke as Governor. Brooke had few specific instructions as to the objects of his government or its possible duration. He was simply told to pacify the Island and establish civil authority, but was given no instruction on creating security forces or on taking steps towards Cuban self-rule.[4]

Into this policy vacuum moved Brigadier General Leonard Wood, Commander of the Department of Santiago. While Brooke and most of the other senior officers in Cuba were aging Civil War veterans (including ex-Confederate General Fitzhugh Lee), Wood was still under forty. Educated as a physician, he had risen with incredible speed from Captain to Brigadier General, helped by his close ties to President McKinley and Theodore Roosevelt. This, combined with his tendency to seek new options rather than sticking to traditional practices, produced considerable friction with Brooke and other officers, but also led to his replacement of Brooke as Military Governor.[5]

One of Wood's innovative policies involved the creation of a mounted rural guard in his department. Most of those recruited were white veterans of the Cuban revolutionary army. Other Department Commanders eventually followed Wood's example. In most cases, Cuban veterans became the unit commanders.[6]

Washington was generally pleased with Wood's efforts, in part because it facilitated American troop withdrawals. Secretary of War Russell A. Alger was especially enthusiastic, urging the recruiting of constabulary forces for urban as well as rural duties not only in Cuba, but in Puerto Rico and the Philippines as well.[7] Washington's enthusiasm was at least in part engendered by its reading of the British experience in Egypt and elsewhere and by the image of Mexico's *Rurales* who had a reputation for turning bandits into rural mounted police.[8] Elihu Root, who had replaced Alger as Secretary of War, believed that a rural guard would "dispose of a lot of men most likely to make trouble in Cuba, turn them from possible bandits, and educate them into Americans."[9]

When Wood replaced Brooke as Military Governor he was able to combine the separate Rural Guard units into a single, national force. While almost all the officers would be Cubans the American military remained in control of training and administration. The formal structuring of the Guard waited until 5 April 1901 when Wood issued Military Order 114. This created a force of four regiments each commanded by a Cuban lieutenant colonel under the overall command of a Cuban colonel. Considerable authority, however, continued to reside in a US Army Captain, Herbert Slocum, who was appointed as Superintendent of the Rural Guard, with responsibilities for training and organization.[10] A small artillery unit, based in Havana's forts was added to the Guard. By 1902, when the first elected Cuban president took office and the American Army withdrew, the Guard had reached a strength of 1,600 officers and men and Wood believed that they were capable of enforcing the law and maintaining the peace. The final turnover to Cuban control went smoothly, in good part because both the funding and the officers were already Cuban. While an American military advisor remained he had little power and the Guard became essentially a Cuban controlled force. The new president, Tomás Estrada Palma, gave his assurances that the Guard would remain professional and above politics.[11] Both his assurances and Wood's faith would all too soon be proven wrong.

There had been some debate as to whether the Guard, alone, was a sufficient military force. Many Cubans advocated the creation of a regular army alongside the Guard. There was, however, little support for this idea within the American military establishment. This may have been due, in part, to the controversy surrounding Washington's insistence that, as a condition for ending its occupation, Cuba incorporate into its Constitution and ratify a treaty containing the provisions of the Platt Amendment which the US Congress had added to the 1901 Army Appropriations Bill. Among the Amendment's provisions were a prohibition on any other nation acquiring bases in Cuba, a Cuban obligation to lease naval bases to the United States, and the specific right of American military intervention "for the preservation of Cuban independence, the maintenance of a government adequate for the protection of life, property, and liberty.[12] In later writings Senator Orville H. Platt, the amendment's author, noted that, "the new government of Cuba will have neither an army nor a navy," and expressed his belief that the US naval bases and the explicit right of intervention "will prevent trouble there."[13]

The Platt Amendment virtually insured that neither the Army nor the Navy would favor creation of a Cuban regular army. Should the U.S. decide to exercise its right to intervene such a force might provide armed resistance. With the Navy determined to maintain a permanent presence in Cuba and initially hoping for much more than just the base at Guantanamo, they too might be called upon to intervene and had no desire to confront a Cuban army.[14] President Palma seemed to echo their sentiments declaring, "We should have a degree of order such that the Army would become unnecessary."[15]

For most of President Palma's first term things seemed to go fairly well. The Rural Guard, which had grown to over 3,000, enforced order in the countryside and a National Police patrolled the cities. There were occasional outbreaks of violence, notably when the Guard and police were used against labor strikes, but most of the nation remained relatively peaceful.[16] But the situation rapidly deteriorated in 1905 as Cuba's next round of elections approached.

Determined to hold on to power, Palma set about rigging the elections. Unsure of the Guard's personal loyalty, he expanded the Artillery Corps and placed it directly under his command. It would prove ineffective when, in 1906, the opposition Liberals, who had boycotted the elections, began a revolt. While the resulting uprising included more political maneuvering than actual fighting, the government's position steadily deteriorated. There were some clashes between rebels and the Rural Guard, but there were also numerous defections of Guard units.[17] As the conflict spread it became apparent that both sides were counting more on American intervention than on a military victory.

This placed President Theodore Roosevelt on the horns of a dilemma. He could not let the conditions on the island continue to deteriorate but he wanted to avoid intervention. In a 9 September 1906 letter, he expressed his frustration:

> I have just been notified by the Cuban government that they intend to ask us forcibly to intervene in the course of this week, and I have sent them a most emphatic protest against their doing so, with a statement that I am not prepared to say what I will do if the request is made. On the one hand we can not see Cuba permanently a prey to misrule and anarchy; on the other hand I loath the thought of assuming any control over the island such as we have over Porto Rico or the Philippines. We emphatically do not want it.[18]

Roosevelt's efforts to avoid intervention ultimately proved futile. On 14 September, he ordered powerful Naval forces and a Marine battalion to Cuban waters and had the Marine Corps prepare additional units for possible intervention. He also dispatched Secretary of War William Howard Taft and Assistant Secretary of State Robert Bacon to Cuba in an effort to negotiate a political settlement. But with both sides preferring American intervention to making any concessions to their opponents, the mission was doomed to failure.[19]

Shortly after Taft and Bacon arrived, President Palma suddenly resigned and his Vice President refused to replace him. With no Cuban government, Taft authorized the landing of 2,000 Marines and proclaimed a provisional government administered by the United States with himself as Governor.[20] The Marine Brigade quickly fanned out across the island, insuring that the opposing armed forces were kept separate and that relative peace was restored. The Marine Corps, however, had no intention of taking on an extended occupation. That task would once again fall to the Army.

The Marines stayed long enough to disarm many of the Cubans, but left within a few weeks as Army units arrived. Ultimately, over 6,000 US troops would serve in this second occupation of Cuba, but many would have little to do as there would be no significant clashes between American and Cuban forces. Indeed things became so peaceful that many officers brought their families to Cuba where their salaries procured a much more comfortable lifestyle, complete with servants, than they could expect to enjoy at home.[21]

Taft only remained as Governor for a few weeks as he had to return to his duties as Secretary of War. In his place, Roosevelt appointed a civilian bureaucrat with experience in Panama, Charles E. Magoon.[22] Honest, dedicated, but uninspiring, Magoon saw his task as creating, as soon as possible, conditions which would enable the United States to return the government to the Cubans. He was determined to minimize conflicts with Cuba's political elites and was little concerned with the long-range impact of his policies on Cuba.

An urgent task was insuring that Cuban forces would be able to maintain control over future internal political disturbances. One of the first decisions was to retain the Rural Guard, including its commander, but to reform and reequip it, making a more effective force. In their report of their mission to Cuba, Taft and Bacon concluded that the weakness and wide dispersal of the Guard had "left the government naked to its enemies and critics," and "utterly unprepared to meet this attack.[23] Making the Guard more effective while, at the same time, keeping it separate from politics would not prove an easy task. The Guard had become politicized under Palma, cooperating in insuring his victory in the 1905 election, and then had not performed well against the subsequent uprising.[24] In an effort to divorce the Guard from Cuban politics Magoon issued a decree making political activity by Guard personnel a court-martial offense and the Guard's Cuban Commander issued a General Order: "The members of the armed forces will not discuss, either publicly or privately, their political opinions. They are soldiers of the state and as such have no right to mix in politics. Their duty is to serve their government and take no part in its construction. . . . The welfare of the entire force depends on its being free from political combinations."[25]

To undertake the task of reforming the Guard the Army called upon several veterans of the Wood era, notably Major Herbert Slocum who had earlier been the Guard's Superintendent. Slocum and his fellow officers believed the Guard had to be expanded and have more of its force stationed near major population centers so that it could quickly respond to any uprisings. They also favored making more promotions from the ranks.[26] Despite never having more than eight other American officers to assist him, Slocum did manage to accomplish quite a bit. Guard weapons and training were improved, the ranks culled, and modern communications installed in many posts. The force was steadily expanded, in 1907 reaching a strength of over 5,000 divided into three regiments. Discipline and morale improved steadily, something the Americans attributed to the officers exhibiting greater concern for the welfare of the enlisted men.[27] The Guard undertook expanded rural patrols as well as continuing to enforce routine law and order.[28] An abortive revolutionary plot in 1907 was quickly discovered and defused, more by the Havana Police than by the Guard, and the occupation continued to be basically peaceful. By the end of 1907, the force seemed well on its way to becoming the professional, largely nonpolitical force that its American founders had always envisioned. When Magoon included a list of the principle problems facing Cuba in his Annual Report, issued in January 1908, there were no military or security issues on the list.[29]

Once again, however, the realities of Cuba's political culture would disrupt the American's carefully constructed plans. Much of the leadership of both the Liberal and Conservative Parties opposed expansion of the Guard and argued that Cuba should instead create a regular army. Confident of victory in the 1908 elections, the Liberals were especially insistent that only a regular army could crush revolutionary outbreaks at their inception. They also argued that an infantry force would be less costly than an expanded, mounted Guard and that only if it had an army could Cuba be considered a truly sovereign state.[30] This last argument conveniently omitted the fact that so long as the Platt Amendment remained in force Cuban sovereignty would be limited at best.

Magoon and the American officers attached to the Guard were less than enthusiastic about the idea of a regular army, fearing, as it turned out correctly, that such a force might prove easy prey to political influences. But the Cuban advocates of an army were unrelenting, using the press to criticize the Guard and argue for a regular Army. The debate lasted into 1908. With an election approaching and the expectation that American withdrawal would soon follow, Washington essentially gave in, demonstrating that ending the occupation rather than Cuba's long-range future was its first priority.

A plan, advanced by Roosevelt and Taft, called for an expansion of the Guard, but also the creation of a brigade of regular infantry. The Army could later be expanded by taking in some units of the Guard. The Cuban Constitution was also to be modified to create a militia that could be called out in case of need. American officers would have little part in the training of the army nor would the United States have much influence in selecting its officers. There was little effort to pretend that the selection of officers, especially for the senior ranks, would be nonpolitical. This was underlined when Magoon acquiesced in the Liberal's choice for Army commander, General Faustino, a leader of the 1906 Liberal revolt, known largely for not taking prisoners.[31]

The American officers attached to the Guard were upset by these developments, but were powerless to alter them. They correctly foresaw that the Cuban Army would become a political instrument and that the Guard would be hard pressed not to follow the same path.[32] With Washington set on a rapid withdrawal all they could do was finalize their training efforts and hope they would not have to return at some future date to again undertake a similar task.

One American officer, Captain Frank Parker, was detailed to remain behind as advisor to the Rural Guard and another, Captain George Gately, filled a similar function with the Cuban Artillery. Parker's instructions urged him to be "discreet" and "useful," but said nothing about trying to keep the Guard apolitical.[33] It is probably unlikely that any efforts he might have made in that direction would have had any effect, but the record indicates that his influence actually helped politicize the guard. He devoted his major effort to making it a military-oriented cavalry force, useful largely in discouraging political opposition. Ultimately, the Guard's best unit became the personal guard of the President and the rest came increasingly under the control of officers known more for their political loyalties than their military skills. Discipline deteriorated and by 1912 the number of courts-martial was greater than the Guard's enlisted strength.[34]

As the Guard deteriorated the Army expanded. By 1909–1910, the Army and Guard's combined strength had reached 404 officers and 8,772 enlisted men.[35] Six years later, the authorized strength of the Guard was only 5,508 while that of the Army had reached 11,715 men.[36] By then, the Guard had come under the command of the Army's senior officers and had become a political instrument of the ruling party. In the 1916 elections, it played a major role in insuring that the desired results were obtained.

In 1912, American troops had returned to Cuba but this time not as an occupying force. Long discriminated against and increasingly frustrated by the elites' political domination, some Afro-Cubans had tried to organize an "Independent Party of Color." When this predictably got nowhere, some of its members turned to armed revolt. In most areas, combined Army-Guard forces were able to quickly defeat the insurgents, but the American Minister to Cuba, Arthur M. Beaupre was so alarmed that he cabled the State Department that the revolt "will not be put down for months or even years without material assistance or intervention by the American government."[37]

Marines from Guantánamo, joined by detachments from several warships, entered Cuba and were largely assigned to protect American property owners. But the Cuban government needed no assistance in ending

24

the rebellion and Washington saw no need to involve itself with their military operations. The Marines were soon withdrawn. A few years later, they were back.

What was happening was that the United States was increasingly becoming the supporter of governments that used the now totally politicized Army and Guard to manipulate elections and crush opposition. The vision of an apolitical force that would both maintain stability and support at least some form of democratic government had virtually disappeared. Personal ambition, more than any ideology, had come to dominate Cuban politics. In 1916, the government was nominally Conservative, but splits in both major parties made this nearly meaningless. The election evolved into a fight by incumbent President Mario Menocal to hold on to power. When the returns appeared to be going against him he simply resorted to open fraud and proclaimed his reelection. When neither the Central Electoral Board nor the Supreme Court upheld this, supplementary elections were scheduled in two provinces. But before they could be held a group of Army officers tried to overthrow Menocal. Many senior officers owed heir appointments to the previous Liberal government and were openly sympathetic to that party. Others were evidently upset at the extent of government fraud, combined with efforts to arm the regime's civilian supporters. Those plotting against the government expected at least 75 percent of the military to join them. They were wrong. Their plans were discovered and their leaders arrested.[38] Liberal Party supporters then launched their own uprising.[39] Many apparently hoped that this might force US intervention. But, with much of the Army occupied on the Mexican border and the prospect of war with Germany looming the Wilson administration was in no position to dispatch large units to Cuba. Instead Washington shipped arms and ammunition to the Cuban government and landed small forces at several coastal points, releasing Cuban forces to battle the insurgents.[40]

By this time, the United States had apparently lost all interest in or hope of having a professional, nonpolitical constabulary or army in Cuba. Its concerns focused on curbing German activities on the island and, once war with Germany began, protecting the sugar crop. As Liberal guerrillas began burning sugar fields, probably hoping this might force intervention, the United States and Cuba arrived at a strange formula whereby the United States would request and Cuba would grant the use of its territory for training Marines. Why tropical Cuba was a desirable site for training units that might be destined for Europe was never explained. Ultimately, nearly 3,000 Marines spent the war in Cuba, camped near American sugar properties, and freeing the Cuban Army to destroy the last vestiges of armed opposition. After the war, this force was slowly reduced, though one battalion remained until 1922.[41] Meanwhile, the Cuban Army continued to expand. As a last vestige of American influence, over 150 officers were given train- ing in the United States. This improved their professional skills, but also made their political loyalties suspect and they were largely excluded from key commands.

While the Rural Guard continued to exist, it had, by the 1920s, lost most of its separate identity and was basically the cavalry arm of the Cu- ban Army. During the dictatorship of Gerardo Machado, 1925–1933, its units were used against student protests, labor strikes, and assorted efforts to overthrow the regime. Not trusting officers who had been trained in the United States, Machado began promoting officers from the ranks.[42] This created a faction loyal to him, but at the same time increased the discontent of the US-trained officers and of the sergeants who did not receive such promotions. As Machado's tyranny increased and opposition, much of it from the left, grew increasingly violent, the United States dispatched a special envoy, Sumner Welles, to attempt to resolve the situation without military intervention. Ultimately, the Army, certainly with Welles encour- agement, if not his active participation, forced Machado into exile.[43]

Stability seemed to be returning until early September 1933, when the sergeants at Camp Columbia, Havana's key military base, revolted. Led by Sergeant Fulgencio Batista, they allied with a reformist political movement, took over the government, and began purging the Army, ultimately replacing 512 officers with enlisted men, warrant officers and a few civilians.[44] Many of the removed officers, together with some colleagues still technically on active duty, gathered together in Havana's National Hotel, seeking ways to reverse the revolt and/or to promote US intervention. Batista, who had made himself a colonel and army chief of staff, ordered his artillery to shell the hotel. After two days of sporadic fighting the officers gave up.[45] This marked the destruction of the last vestiges of US influence over Cuba's military and the beginning of Fulgencio Batista's domination of politics. That would last until the end of 1958 when Fidel Castro destroyed Batista's army and began his own prolonged rule.

The American effort to form a nonpolitical, constabulary must be judged as a failure. In part this was because US control over events in Cuba was always partial and of limited duration. The Cuban political elites played on American desires to withdraw from Cuba and on Washington's fear of internal disorders first to influence the development of the Rural Guard and then to make it subordinate to a clearly political (and probably unnecessary) army. From its inception the bulk of the officers, including

26

the higher ranks, were Cuban. While this facilitated the US withdrawal it also insured that Cuban politics were imbedded in the Guard from its inception. Most senior officers were revolutionary army veterans with little US training and strong personal ties to political factions.

The Platt Amendment, designed to enshrine American influence in Cuba, proved to have an opposite effect. Cuban factions constantly maneuvered to create conditions that might compel US intervention while the U.S. increasingly sought to avoid such a contingency. This made Washington willing to tolerate violent political repression. When the Amendment was finally abrogated in May 1934 it gave American policymakers new options. Unfortunately, the abrogation came much too late to have any impact on the destruction of the Rural Guard.

Notes

1. Rafael Fermoselle, *The Evolution of the Cuban Military, 1492–1986* (Miami, FL: Ediciones Universal, 1987), 94–95.

2. David F. Healy, *The United States in Cuba, 1898–1902: Generals, Politicians and the Search for Policy* (Madison, WI: The University of Wisconsin Press, 1963), 69–77.

3. Freddy L. Polk, "Building Armies for Democracy: U.S. Attempts to Reform the Armed Forces of Cuba (1906–1909) and Nicaragua (1927–1933)" (Master of Military Art and Science Thesis, US Army Command and General Staff College, Fort Leavenworth, KS, 1987), 35; Fermoselle, 96; Louis A. Pérez Jr., *Cuba Under the Platt Amendment, 1902–1934* (Pittsburgh, PA: University of Pittsburgh Press, 1986), 149.

4. James Harrison Wilson, *Under the Old Flag: Recollections of Military Operations in the War for the Union, the Spanish War, the Boxer Rebellion, Etc.*, Vol. II (New York, NY: D. Appleton & Co., 1912), 479–480.

5. Healy, 65–66; Wilson, Vol. II, 497.

6. Fermoselle, 95.

7. Allan R. Millett, "The Rise and Fall of the Cuban Rural Guard, 1898–1912," *The Americas*, Vol. 29, No. 2 (October 1972), 192.

8. For a history of the *Rurales,* see Paul J. Vanderwood, *Disorder and Progress: Bandits, Police and Mexican Development* (Lincoln, NE: University of Nebraska Press, 1981).

9. Elihu Root to William McKinley, 17 August 1899, quoted in Millett, "Rise and Fall," 192.

10. Fermoselle, 95 and 103.

11. Millett, "Rise and Fall," 196.

12. For the text of the Platt Amendment, along with many other relevant documents, see Robert F. Smith, *What Happened in Cuba: A Documentary History* (New York, NY: Twayne Publishers, 1963), 125–132.

13. Senator Orville H. Platt to Edwin F. Atkins, "Senator Orville H. Platt on Relations with Cuba, May 1901," 11 June 1901, in *An Old Fashioned Senator: Orville H. Platt of Connecticut* by Louis Arthur Coolidge (New York, NY: G.P. Putnam's Sons, 1910), 314; Smith, 128–129.

14. For a description of Navy efforts to acquire additional bases and Cuban opposition to this, see Richard D. Challener, *Admirals, Generals, and American Foreign Policy* (Princeton, NJ: Princeton University Press, 1973), 94–100.

15. Quoted in Fermoselle, 99.

16. Ibid., 105–106.

17. Millett, "Rise and Fall," 198.

18. Theodore Roosevelt to George Otto Trevelyan, 9 September 1906; Smith, 137.

19. Allan R. Millett, *The Politics of Intervention: The Military Occupation of Cuba, 1906–1909* (Columbus, OH: The Ohio State University Press, 1968), 78–79.

20. Hugh Thomas, *Cuba, The Pursuit of Freedom* (New York, NY: Harper and Row, 1971), 477–480.

21. Allan R. Millett, *The General: Robert L. Bullard and Officership in the United States Army, 1881–1925* (Westport, CT: Greenwood, 1975), 196.

22. For a description of Magoon's previous career, see David A. Lockmiller, *Magoon in Cuba* (Chapel Hill, NC: The University of North Carolina Press, 1938), 73–76; Millett, *Politics of Intervention*, 150. Millett asserts that many of Magoon's subsequent problems "would have been lessened had he worn a uniform and acted as Cubans thought a ruler should."

23. Quoted in Pérez, *Cuba Under the Platt Amendment*, 105–106.

24. Polk, 43.

25. Republic of Cuba, Headquarters of the Armed Forces, General Order 28, 11 March 1907, quoted in Millett, "Rise and Fall," 199.

26. Polk, 45.

27. Millett, *Politics of Intervention*, 225.

28. Millett, "Rise and Fall," 199–200.

29. Millett, *Politics of Intervention*, 192–193.

30. Polk, 47.

31. Ibid., 51.

32. Millett, "Arise and Fall," 204–205; Polk, 51–52; Lester D. Langley, *Banana Wars: An Inner History of American Empire, 1900–1934* (Lexington, KY: The University Press of Kentucky, 1983), 48–49.

33. Millett, "Rise and Fall," 208.

34. Ibid., 209–210.

35. Fermoselle, 113.

36. *Memoria de la Administracion del Presidente de la Republica de Cuba, Mayor General Mario G. Menocal, durante el periodo Comprendido entre el 1 de Julio, de 1915 y el 30 de Junio, 1916* (Havana, Cuba: Secretaria de la Presidencia, 1919), 153–170.

37. Arthur Beaupre to the Secretary of State, 8 June 1912, *Papers Relating to the Foreign Relations of the United States* (Washington, DC: Government Printing Office, 1919), 253.

38. This was the first attempt at military revolt by significant elements of the armed forces, but would be far from the last.

39. Louis A. Pérez, Jr., *Intervention, Revolution, and Politics in Cuba, 1913–1921* (Pittsburgh, PA: University of Pittsburgh Press, 1978), 22–27.

40. Pérez, *Cuba Under the Platt Amendment*, 169–170.

41. Allan R. Millett, *Semper Fidelis: A History of the United States Marine Corps* (Second edition) (New York, NY: The Free Press, 1992), 130.

42. Thomas, 582–583.

43. Bryce Wood, *The Making of the Good Neighbor Policy* (New York, NY: Columbia University Press, 1961), 62–69.

44. Fermoselle, 152.

45. Justo Carillo, *Cuba, 1933: estudiantes, yanquis y soldados* (Miami, FL: Instituto de Estudios Interamericanos, University of Miami, 1985), 288–295; Thomas, 6.

Chapter 4

Panama: More Issues Than Running a Canal

U.S. dealings with Panama have always been distinct from those involving other Western Hemisphere nations. Key to this has been that nation's location as a trans-isthmian route for people and commerce. From the California gold rush of 1849 to the present day, the United States has been determined to have unfettered access to that route and concerned about other nations' real or imagined designs on it. In the first decade of the 20th century, when Panama broke away from Colombia and the United States determined to build a canal through the new nation, Washington's concerns with and involvement in internal affairs escalated dramatically.

Panama was the last Latin American nation to achieve independence and, like Cuba, did so in good part because of US intervention. It, however, differed from Cuba, and from the Philippines, in that there had been no armed struggle for independence and there was no revolutionary army to pose an obstacle either to US interests or to the domestic political elite. In addition, shortly after independence, the United States took control of the Canal Zone, a strip of territory that divided Panama, and stationed a permanent garrison there. In the process it assumed basic responsibility not only for the security of the Canal, but for that of Panama as well. No nation in Latin America was subject to greater US influence and, with the possible exception of Mexico, in no nation was American strategic and commercial interests so important.

While Panama did not have its own army in 1903, it inherited one. The commander of Colombian forces on the Isthmus, General Esteban Huertas, was persuaded, by a combination of American threats and Panamanian bribes, to change sides and his garrison briefly became the Army of Panama.[1] From its inception this force was controversial. Panama had no real frontiers that it needed to defend. It was separated from Colombia on the south by a large expanse of virtually impenetrable jungle. On the north it bordered Costa Rica, which had only a tiny army, and, along with Uruguay, was the most democratic and pacific nation in Latin America. The Hay-Bunau-Varilla Treaty, which created the Canal Zone, also gave the United States the obligation to defend Panamanian independence.[2] The following year Panama adopted its first Constitution which included a clause, similar to one in Cuba's Constitution, giving the United States the right to intervene in order to maintain order.[3] Panamanian newspapers soon began criticizing the Army and the US Minister to Panama, William Buchanan, suggested that it should be transformed into a *Guardia Rural* like the one being created in Cuba. He added, "the men should be armed only with revolvers and spread around the Republic so that no faction might use them collectively to intimidate the government."[4]

Relations between Panama's new government and General Huertas deteriorated steadily. He began to take sides in politics and the Panamanian National Assembly, the nation's unicameral Congress, responded by passing a law reducing the army from 500 to 250 officers and men. Tensions escalated and coup rumors began to circulate. The American Minister was absent, but the Chargé, Joseph Lee, bluntly informed Huertas' political supporters that the United States would not tolerate revolutionary activities. At the same time he cabled the State Department that the Army would be a source of unrest and political upheaval as long as it existed. He also pointed out that the Army was a weak force with some of its soldiers as young as eleven.[5]

Huertas, however, was not discouraged. He continued to try to force the president to alter his cabinet, focusing his opposition on the appointment of Santiago de la Guardia as Minister of War and Foreign Affairs. The president, Manuel Amador, vacillated, but ultimately pressures from both the United States and De la Guardia convinced him that the Army should be abolished. This advice was strengthened by the presence of American naval vessels in Panamanian waters. Their commander, Rear Admiral C.F. Goodrich, further stiffened the president's resolve by placing a company of Marines in proximity to Panama City. Huertas was forced to resign and, after some tense moments and with a repeated threat of US intervention, the army disbanded.[6] Some troops were absorbed into the National Police that had been created the previous year and, to the relief of both the United States and Panama's government, the danger of military interference in politics was, at least for the moment, eliminated.[7]

From 1904 through 1914, while the Canal was being constructed, Washington demonstrated little interest in security conditions in the interior of Panama. What attention existed was focused on the cities of Colón and Panama City at either end of the Canal Zone. Here, predictably, there were numerous clashes between Panamanian police and Americans, largely military, especially around the bars and houses of prostitution in Coco Grove. On several occasions Americans were badly beaten.[8] American ability to respond to these and other incidents was hampered by the unclear division of authority between American diplomatic personnel and the authorities in the Canal Zone, most of who came from the Army Corps of Engineers. In an effort to deal with this, the positions of American Minister to Panama and Canal Zone Governor were briefly combined. Panama's

Foreign Minister, De la Guardia, had agreed to this and, in 1905, Charles Magoon, formerly legal counsel to the Canal Commission (ICC), took the combined position.[9] He held it until he was sent to Cuba as Military Governor in September 1906. The posts were soon separated again and with the appointment of then Major George Goethals to the position of head of the ICC and Chief Engineer the officials in the Zone began to take over much of the policy formulation process from the State Department and the diplomatic mission. This would be especially true when security issues were involved.

Meanwhile, clashes between the Panamanian police and Americans and canal construction workers continued with a major riot breaking out in 1906. An attempt to have a New York police official take over training the force lasted only a few weeks. Magoon's successor as Minister, Herbert Squiers, wanted to take away high-powered rifles from the police and to totally reorganize the courts, the police, and the prison system.[10] This did not happen. Instead the United States relied on the presence of the Marines and the threat of intervention to keep matters from getting completely out of hand. At the same time, the Americans built up their own police force in the Zone, consisting of a unit of 117 white Americans and another of 116 West Indians. The former was responsible for maintaining order among the Zone's Caucasian residents and for dealing with Panamanians arrested inside the zone, the latter dealt with the non-white labor force.[11] Few of either group spoke Spanish and neither did most judges who tried Panamanians arrested inside the Zone.[12] Not surprisingly, this further exacerbated tensions between Panamanians and Zone authorities.

The August 1914 opening of the Canal coincided with the outbreak of the World War I in Europe. Concerns over Canal security increased rapidly and began to encompass developments throughout Panama. In 1911, the first Army infantry unit had arrived in the Zone and the Army steadily replaced the Navy as the service primarily responsible for security. By 1912, the Navy was even arguing that the zone be governed by an Army officer "who combines in his own person the functions of military command and civil control."[13]

Panamanian authorities were increasingly concerned about the clashes between the police and Americans and worried that this might provide an excuse to establish an American military government. On 29 April 1915, Panama's Foreign Minister, E.T. Lefevre wrote Governor Goethals, now a Brigadier General, asking him "to obtain through your intermediation an instructor for our National Police." He continued:

Nearly all the governments of the Republic, more or less, have tried to acquire the services of American instructors to improve our Police Department, but unfortunately in the field of practice, these efforts have not always given the desired results . . . A contract was entered into with a Mr. Jimenez who was a member of the Police Department of New York . . . There were suspicions the he protected certain interests which the police were bound to prosecute. The scandal caused by the revelations which resulted therefrom was the cause of the cancellation of the respective contract. . . . Later . . . arrangements were made for another instructor, a Mr. Clarke. This gentleman . . . might have been a good military instructor, on the other hand he did not possess the energy nor the knowledge of police affairs indispensible to organize the Panamanian Police as was required, and this new attempt failed.

After detailing yet another failed attempt involving an Army Major Helfert, who also lacked experience in police matters and resigned, Lefevre concluded:

Among the extensive personnel of the Zone officials there must be someone who knowing our customs and our language, and appreciating us, possesses the necessary knowledge in order to serve as instructor of the Panamanian Police. When this person has been found we will take care of the rest and the sincere desire which the President has . . . of making of our Police Department a model of its kind should contribute greatly to the success of the mission of the new instructor.[14]

Two months later the Acting Governor of the Canal Zone, Colonel Chester Harding, replied, offering the services of a Lieutenant L.A. McIntire, but with numerous conditions attached. These included his being given the rank of Inspector and having four assistants appointed from the Zone Police, each with the rank of Captain and with authority over all but two members of the existing police. He also demanded:

To have entire charge and control of the Police Force, under the Comandante of Police, and to be responsible for the instruction and discipline of the members thereof, which authority shall include specifically: Sole authority to suspend summarily and member of the Police Force other that the Comandante of Police. . . . Sole authority to employ and assign to duty of members of the Police Force. Sole charge of the investigation of complaints against members of the Police Force.[15]

While negotiations over McIntire's possible appointment dragged on a major crisis erupted between the National Police and Zone authorities. In early 1915 there were two major clashes between Panamanians and members of the American military, in the second of which up to 1500 American troops engaged in a riot in the city of Colón after an American corporal was killed. Goethals wanted the US Army to take over policing duties in Panama City and Colón, but was overruled by General Leonard Wood. Panama proposed recruiting Americans to patrol the red light districts, but Goethals rejected this idea.[16] The stalemate was broken in early 1916 when the United States found an excuse to demand that the Panamanian Police be disarmed of their high-powered rifles. Panama's government protested bitterly, but could only get an exception made for the tiny Presidential Guard. The State Department also demanded an indemnity for the American killed, but a Panamanian court cleared the police of responsibility and no indemnity was ever paid.[17] A few months later a senior Zone official wrote, "The arrangement of having a provost guard in the two Panamanian cities and taking away of rifles from the Panamanian police, has made a wonderful improvement in the situation respecting order in the two cities."[18]

While discussions over the appointment of McIntire or some other American to supervise the police continued well into 1917, the American entry into World War I and consequent concerns over Canal defense soon overshadowed all other considerations. Taking advantage of a provision of the Hay-Bunau-Varilla treaty that empowered Washington to take lands for Canal defense, the United States expanded the area under its control and even tried to seize the Panamanian holiday island of Taboga. Panama quickly followed the US lead in declaring war on the Central Powers, but its major role was harassing resident Germans and exporting bananas. In 1918, an American, Albert Lamb of the Washington, DC police, was appointed as an instructor to the Panamanian police and in 1919, following more American pressure, he was made Inspector General with broad powers of control. He held that post until 1924 when Panama's Assembly passed a law returning the force to national control.[19]

No real effort was made by either Panama or the United States to strengthen internal security forces during the war. Instead, the American military expanded its control, taking over Colón and Panama City before the July 1918 presidential elections. Even more controversial was the virtual occupation of Panama's northernmost province, Chiriquí. It began with an uprising in protest of the results of the 1918 election. Without being asked, the United States sent troops to help put down the uprising, but they remained after the uprising was over. In 1920, after Bainbridge Colby replaced Robert Lansing as Secretary of State, the troops were finally withdrawn.[20]

Shortly after WWI ended, Panama had its closest brush with war with a neighbor. US Supreme Court Justice Edward White had apparently settled a lingering dispute over the boundary with Costa Rica through arbitration. The decision strongly favored Costa Rican claims and Panama refused to accept it. In 1921, Costa Rica sent troops to occupy the disputed territory. Despite its lack of an army, Panama responded by sending a larger force to the area and capturing the Costa Ricans. Costa Rica then sent a still larger force into the Panamanian province of Bocas del Toro. Panamanian nationalism was aroused and there was considerable talk of raising an army, but the United States quashed all such ideas and ultimately forced Panama to accept White's decision.[21]

The remainder of the 1920s were relatively uneventful. The police handled routine internal security, and the conflict with Costa Rica helped convince Washington that it did not want Panama to have an army. US officials engaged in internal debates over Canal security, leading to continued annexation of small parcels of Panamanian territory, but relations remained generally peaceful. A revision of the Canal Treaties that removed some commercial irritants but also increased US control was signed in 1926 but never ratified by Panama. That same year the US Navy helped settle a brief uprising by Panama's indigenous Kuna people.[22]

Two developments in the 1930s threatened to disrupt relations. The first was the impact of the world depression. The other was the political ascent of the Arias brothers, Arnulfo and Harmodio. Arnulfo would be a major figure, and a constant source of instability, for the next half century.

First under Herbert Hoover, and then more decisively under Franklin Roosevelt, the United States moved away from intervening in internal Panamanian affairs. While Washington continued to discourage any Panamanian plans for developing their own army, it resisted temptations to use American force to settle political disputes, even refusing to supply Panama's police with tear gas or with any training on its use. As the Commander of American forces in Panama, General Lytle Brown noted, "Any action which might connect the United States Army with the use of gas against a Latin American populace could bring forth throughout Latin America a storm of protest."[23]

In 1936, the Franklin Roosevelt administration negotiated a major revision of the Hay-Bunau-Varilla Treaty. This increased annual payments to Panama and promised equal treatment for US and Panamanian Canal employees. It ended the American right to acquire additional land for Canal defense and, terminated the right to intervene in order to restore order. Although the Senate waited until 1939 to ratify the new treaty, the administration acted as if it was in force and Panama began to lose its protectorate status.[24]

The National Police were also strengthened and began to resemble a constabulary. Some units were mounted and used both to patrol rural areas and to break up labor strikes and student demonstrations in urban areas. The Arias brothers controlled politics and, freed from the threat of US intervention, used the strengthened police to manipulate elections and harass political opponents. A small number of machine guns and automatic rifles were acquired from the US Army in the Zone and a presidential guard was created, apart from and better armed than the police, and used to guard not only the president, but other government buildings.[25]

Arnulfo Arias became president in 1940 and his problems with the United States grew rapidly. He appointed a Guatemalan crony Commandant of the National Police and, in October 1941, refused a US request to allow arming of Panamanian flagged merchant ships. Shortly thereafter, with the approval if not the instigation of the United States, he was overthrown and replace by Ricardo Adolfo de la Guardia. Relations improved, the merchant ships were armed, but when De la Guardia asked for Lend Lease aid he was turned down on the grounds that Panama did not have an army.[26]

During World War II, unlike a quarter of a century earlier, there was a real danger of attacks on the Canal and the United States made a major effort to strengthen its defenses. Over 60,000 military personnel were stationed on 14 bases and at over 100 other defense sites. Numerous sites were acquired from Panama, but were now rented, not simply seized.[27] Aside from maintaining internal order and dealing with resident Axis citizens, no real role was assigned to the Panamanians.

During this period one of the few Panamanians with formal military training, José Antonio Remón, a graduate of the Mexican Military Academy, rose to prominence in the Police. He had clashed with both Arias brothers, being dismissed for several years by Harmodio and then sent to take a cavalry course at Fort Riley by Arnulfo.[28] Shortly after the war he became Police Commandant and used his position to dominate politics.

Panama had created an intelligence unit attached to the police and an FBI official was made technical advisor to this unit, largely to watch the activities of Arnulfo, who had returned from exile and was running for president in 1948.[29] Meanwhile, Remón slowly, but steadily beefed up the military side of the Police and began sending Panamanians abroad for military training, including enrollment in several Latin American military academies. He did this with little help from the United States. From 1946 through 1962, the only military assistance provided Panama was $100,000 for Military Education and Training.[30]

After a period of chaos, Arnulfo Arias returned to the Presidency in 1949. He lasted until 1951 when he tried to dissolve the Assembly and arrest his opponents. Instead Remón and the Police ousted him and the re-constituted Assembly banned him from politics for life. Remón now used his power to manipulate new elections and, in 1952, became president. One of his first acts was to have a law passed which renamed the 2,500 strong Police the National Guard, reflecting its transformation into a constabulary force.[31] Panama also began sending students to US Army training courses held in the Canal Zone at what was originally the US Army Caribbean School and, in 1963, became the School of the Americas. Panama's costs were much lower than other nations since those assigned could stay at home and often were also able to work part-time at their jobs in the Guard. By 1984, 4,202 Panamanians had taken such courses and that was, despite the force's small size, the third highest total in Latin America.[32]

Remón's presidency was both controversial and short. He initiated social reforms and strengthened the new National Guard. The Canal Treaties were modified, increasing payments to Panama, but also giving the United States continued access to military bases in the Republic. He was also accused of large scale corruption and there were even allegations that he was involved in narcotics trafficking, which began going from Bolivia through Panama to the United States while he was president.[33] All of this was cut short in 1955 when he was assassinated. His vice president was accused of complicity, but neither he nor anyone else was ever tried or convicted.

Remón's death inaugurated a renewed period of turmoil. Inspired by Egypt's seizure of the Suez Canal, students and others began a series of anti-American demonstrations that the Guard, at first, violently suppressed. Both fearful of future events and desirous of not creating martyrs the US Embassy urged providing the Guard with nonlethal riot control equipment including tear gas.[34] In 1959, there were also two attempts at exile invasions, one of which included a group of Cubans. With American concerns over Fidel Castro's rule in Cuba rising, this contributed to a major shift in support for the Guard. US military assistance began to flow in 1962 and over the next eighteen years totaled $15 million.[35]

A major crisis in US–Panamanian relations broke out in January 1964 when Panamanian students tried to have their flag flown at Balboa High School in the Zone. Three days of rioting followed leaving three American soldiers and at least twenty Panamanians dead. During most of the rioting the Guard stood aside, protecting the US Embassy, but not other property and doing nothing to discourage the rioters.[36] In the aftermath, Panama broke relations with the United States and demanded that the Canal Treaties be renegotiated.

These events inaugurated a prolonged period of negotiations that culminated in the 1977 Carter-Torrijos Treaties. Domestic politics in both nations prolonged the process, as did American preoccupation with the Vietnam War and the Watergate scandals. In Panama deteriorating relations between the Guard and civilian politicians reached a boiling point when Arnulfo Arias was returned to the presidency in the 1968 elections. When Arias attempted to alter the Guard's command structure, a group of dissident officers, headed by Colonel Omar Torrijos and Major Boris Martinez ousted him and again sent him into exile. This, his third and last presidential term, lasted less than eleven days.

Torrijos and Martinez soon fell out and Martinez found himself in exile in Miami. Then another group of officers tried to oust Torrijos, but, with key support from Major Manuel Antonio Noriega, Torrijos held on to power. He would dominate Panama until his 1981 death in a plane crash and the military would rule for another eight years after that.

Under Torrijos, a series of puppet civilian presidents held office, but there was never any doubt where real power resided. He ran an extremely hierarchical military organization. He was the only general. There was only one full colonel and a small group of lieutenant colonels, including Noriega. The Guards military capacity slowly increased, but it was not until 1985, four years after his death, that the London-based International Institute for Strategic Studies included a listing for Panama in its annual publication, *The Military Balance*. That year, Panama was credited with a total force of 12,000, and several aircraft, none of which were designed for combat.[37] Every other Latin American nation, including Costa Rica, which had no army, had been included in earlier editions.

Torrijos proved a master in playing different groups against each other. He made deals with the United States and with the Cubans, with the Drug Enforcement Agency and Colombian narcotics traffickers, with Israel and with the Arabs. In the process he kept Panama free of the guerrilla violence that rocked Colombia and much of Central America. Most significantly, he achieved the dream of most Panamanians: he concluded a Treaty with the United States that provided for the end of the Canal Zone and the transfer of the Canal to Panama.

Civilian opponents of the military's rule tended to blame the United States and claim that Torrijos and Noriega were creations of Washington, DC. As one not untypical account put it:

> As for Panama, it had no real military, so its good neighbor to the north came and supplied one. . . . Panama had no military caste, so the United States began to grow one on the formula Toys plus Training yields Esprit de Corps and Elitism. . . .Whoever it was in Washington who decided to give the Guardia Nacional guns and bullets ought to have been submitted to psychiatric evaluation and, if found sane, shot for treason.[38]

It is true that much of the Guard, including Torrijos and Noriega, received some US training, but they also received training in Latin America. Under Torrijos, potential officers were encouraged to attend Latin American military academies and eventually nearly half the Guard's officers had graduated from these institutions. It was Panamanian politicians who for decades had pleaded for heavier weapons and an expanded force and it was Washington that, more often than not, turned them down. The advent of Castro to power changed the equation and the United States, from 1960 on, supported a stronger Guard, though primary responsibility for defending Panama and the Canal continued to rest with the American military. Panama's security forces, exemplified in the career of Remón, had been engaged in making presidents long before this. The United States acquiesced in military rule in Panama, but there is no indication it desired it.

The signing and eventual ratification of the 1979 Torrijos-Carter treaties meant that, by 2000, Panama would have to undertake primary responsibility for Canal defense, at least on the land. There was never any thought of giving Panama a significant air force or naval capability, but it did need strengthening of its land component. Indeed, having a stronger Guard was for some in the Congress a *sine qua non* of their acceptance of the Treaties. Along with the Treaties, the United States had pledged up to $50 million in Foreign Military Sales Credits to equip the Guard to defend the canal. Much of this was disbursed, reaching a peak of $12 million in 1986, but subsequent conflicts with Panama's dictator, Noriega, led to aid being suspended in 1987 and never fully renewed.[39]

Torrijos was killed in a plane crash in 1981 and, after considerable maneuvering and intrigue, Manuel Antonio Noriega emerged as the Guard's commandant. From the start, his rule generated conflict. He lacked the popular charisma and political skills of Torrijos. He renamed the Guard the Panamanian Defense Forces (PDF) and further strengthened its military capabilities. Noriega, like Torrijos, preferred to rule behind puppet presidents and in 1984 used fraud to engineer the election of international banker Nicholas Barletta who allegedly edged out perennial candidate Arnulfo Arias.[40]

The PDF's 1985 murder of a prominent political critic, Hugo Spadafora, was a sharp break with Panamanian political tradition and both frightened and infuriated the civilian opposition. Barletta wanted the murder investigated, but instead he was forcibly ousted and replaced with Vice President Eric Arturo Delvalle. The United States complained, but, with Washington preoccupied with events elsewhere in Central America, it took no action and military assistance and training continued uninterrupted. The combat capacity of the PDF was increased, notably the Battalion 2000 which, by 1987, included airmobile and airborne companies and a mechanized company. The air and naval component was also expanded with the acquisition of a small fleet of helicopters.[41] Unfortunately, the corruption of the PDF's officer corps also increased, with growing involvement in a variety of criminal enterprises, most notably narcotics trafficking.

In the spring of 1987, Noriega moved to shunt aside his chief rival within the PDF, Colonel Roberto Díaz Herrera. In June 1987, Díaz Herrera struck back, giving interviews to the opposition press in which he outlined a litany of charges against Noriega, including narcotics trafficking, involvement in the Spadafora killing, and rigging the 1984 elections. This led to a series of riots and demonstrations that were forcibly suppressed. It also began a final rupture between Noriega and Washington, DC.[42]

The next 30 months were marked by a steady deterioration in relations between the United States and Panama. General Fred Woerner, who had just taken over as the Commander in Chief of the US Southern Command, tried for over a year to both pressure Noriega to resign and to maintain ties with the PDF. Ultimately, he was unable to accomplish either objective and, in 1989, was replaced by General Maxwell Thurman. During this period there were several unsuccessful plots within the PDF officer corps to oust Noriega. The one that came closest to success occurred in early October 1989, shortly after Thurman took command. A group of Panamanian officers, led by Major Moisés Giroldi, actually took Noriega prisoner. But confusion and indecision, both of the part of the plotters and of American authorities in both Panama and Washington, allowed loyal forces to rescue Noriega who promptly had the plots leaders shot.[43]

After three more months of escalating tensions, the United States invaded Panama and quickly destroyed the PDF.[44] This, however, left Panama with no police force and the US military was loath to undertake this task on a long-term basis. A civilian government had been hurriedly installed and First Vice President Ricardo Arias Calderón undertook the difficult talk of creating a new National Police, the Panamanian Public Force (PPF). Overall control was firmly vested in the civilian Ministry of Government and Justice, which Arias Calderón also headed, but the great majority of the manpower, both officers and enlisted, came from remnants of the old PDF.[45] While distasteful to many, this was done because of the urgency of raising a police force and because of the fear of the impact of adding all the old PDF troops into Panama's large number of unemployed. Most of the PDF's higher leadership was forcibly retired with Noriega himself being shipped to the United States for trial. A few officers who had survived earlier plots against Noriega became the initial force commanders, but in short order all were either implicated in earlier criminal actions or involved in efforts to exercise influence over the government and were dismissed. The remnants of the small air and naval units were reorganized, and a Presidential Guard was separated from the police and placed under the Ministry of the Presidency.[46]

The new government was determined to avoid any repeat of previous military dominance of government. A 1992 referendum on Constitutional reform included a prohibition on the creation of an army, articles giving the president extensive powers over the police and the Assembly control over all security budgets, including fixing the number of personnel, and making a civilian head of the PPF with the authority to discipline officers and enlisted men for insubordination.[47] The referendum, however, was overwhelmingly defeated, largely because of political issues not connected to the military reforms. In 1994, an article prohibiting a regular army was added to the Constitution, through a deal between outgoing President Guillermo Endara and his successor Ernesto Pérez Balladares. The article, passed by two successive sessions of the National Assembly, also prohibited members of the Public Force from making political declarations or participating in political protests and made them answerable to provincial and municipal as well as national authorities.[48]

The United States has provided limited training and other assistance to the new PPF. Over time their military capabilities have slowly increased, in part because of intrusions across their southern border by Colombian guerrillas, paramilitaries, and narcotics traffickers. But the under-armed PPF has generally been reluctant to confront such forces, adopting a policy that might be characterized as strategic avoidance. The PPF remains under firm civilian control. Panama still has no military academy, narcotics trafficking through the nation continues, and defense of the Canal depends more on international diplomacy and the US Navy than on the capacity of Panama's security forces.

The Panamanian constabulary was never really a US creation. For decades, Washington expanded greater efforts trying to discourage the formation of such a force than it did in arming and training one. But wider considerations related to the Cold War, Central American conflicts, and most notably the 1977 Canal Treaties reversed this position. Considerable effort was expanded from the late 1960s through the mid-1980s in increasing the military capacity of what became the PDF. But, when a crisis developed over the political domination and rampant corruption of that force, American authorities discovered that their influence was much less than they expected. Ultimately, the US military was called on to destroy the PDF, creating a security vacuum that has still not been adequately filled.

Notes

1. Steve C. Ropp, *Panamanian Politics: From Guarded Nation to National Guard* (New York, NY: Praeger, 1982), 16.

2. For a description of the Treaty and its negotiation, see David McCullough, *The Path Between the Seas* (New York, NY: Simon and Schuster, 1977), 389–396.

3. Sheldon B. Liss, *The Canal: Aspects of United States–Panamanian Relations* (South Bend, IN: University of Notre Dame Press, 1967), 29.

4. Carlos Guevara-Mann, *Panamanian Militarism: A Historical Interpretation* (Athens, OH: Ohio University Press, 1996), 52; William D. McCain, *The United States and the Republic of Panama* (New York, NY: Russell and Russell, 1965), 48–49.

5. Ibid., 51–52.

6. Ibid., 54–59.

7. Guevara-Mann, 54.

8. William Franklin Sands, *Our Jungle Diplomacy* (Chapel Hill, NC: University of North Carolina Press, 1944), 48–51. Sands was an American diplomat in Panama during its first years of independence.

9. Ibid., 60–62; John Major, *Prize Possession: The United States and the Panama Canal, 1903–1979* (Cambridge, UK: Cambridge University Press, 1993), 68–69.

10. Major, 121–22.

11. Michael L. Conniff, *Panama and the United States: The Forced Alliance* (Second Edition) (Athens, GA: The University of Georgia Press, 2001), 75.

12. For a discussion of this, see Henry A. Franck, *Zone Policeman 88* (New York, NY: Arno Press and the New York Times, 1970).

13. Quoted in Major, 72.

14. The Minister of Foreign Affairs of Panama, E.T. Lefevre, to Governor George Goethals, 29 April 1915, Records of the Government of the Canal Zone. I consulted these records in 1966 when they were in a warehouse in Balboa, Canal Zone. They were subsequently moved to the National Archives National Research Center at Suitland, Maryland and classified as RG 185.

15. Colonel Chester Harding to Lefevre, 21 June 1915, RG 185.

16. Major, 133.

17. Ernesto Castillero Pimental, *Panamá y Los Estados Unidos*, Second edition, Panama City, Panama: Editor Humanidad, 1964, 95–99; George W. Baker Jr., "The Wilson Administration and Panama, 1913–1921," *Journal of Inter-American Studies*, Vol. VIII, No. 2 (April 1966), 282–283.

18. Frank Neville to Governor Harding, 9 March 1917, National Archives and Record Service, Records of the Isthmian Canal Commission, 1904–14 and the Panama Canal, 1914–51, RG 185.

19. Guevara-Mann, 56–57.

20. Baker Jr., 290–92. For details on the Chiriquí occupation, see Carlos Cuestas Gómez, *Soldados Americans en Chiriquí* (Panama City, Panama: n.p., 1991).

21. McCain, 206–222.
22. Conniff, 86–87.
23. Major, 251–253.
24. Conniff, 90–91.
25. Major, 257–258.
26. Ibid., 267–269.
27. For a detailed account of defense efforts, see Charles Morris Brooks, *Guarding the Crossroads: Security and Defense of the Panama Canal* (Panama: P & P Group, 2003), 43–198. There were several encounters between Panama-based air and sea units and German U-Boats.
28. Guevara-Mann, 63.
29. Major, 270.
30. Agency for International Development, *US Overseas Loans and Grants and Assistance from International Organizations: Obligations and Loan Authorizations, July 1, 1945–September 30, 1980* (Washington, DC: Government Printing Office, undated), 55.
31. Guevara-Mann, 62.
32. William H. Ormsbee Jr., "U.S. Army School of the Americas (USARSA): Profile of a Training Institution," *DISAM Journal*, Vol. 7, No. 2 (Winter 1984), 88.
33. Larry L. Pippin, *The Remon Era: An Analysis of a Decade of Events in Panama, 1947–1957* (Palo Alto, CA: Stanford University, Institute of Hispanic American and Luso-Brazilian Studies, 1964), 8.
34. Conniff, 112.
35. Agency for International Development, 55.
36. William J. Jorden, *Panama Odyssey* (Austin, TX: University of Texas Press, 1984), 63. For an excellent description of these events, based in part on numerous interviews with participants, see Chris Swilling, "The High Price of Neglect: The 1964 Flag Crisis in Panama" (M.A. thesis, Southern Illinois University–Edwardsville, 1993).
37. The International Institute for Strategic Studies, *The Military Balance, 1985–1986* (London, UK: The International Institute for Strategic Studies, 1985), 153.
38. R.M. Koster and Guillermo Sanchez, *In the Time of the Tyrants: Panama, 1968–1990* (New York, NY: W.W. Norton and Co., 1990), 57–58.
39. Steve Ropp, "National Security," in *Panama: A Country Study*, ed. By Sandra W. Meditz, Dennis Hanrath and Dennis Michael Hanratty. (Washington, D.C.: US Government Printing Office, 1989), 127.
40. Margaret Scranton, *The Noriega Years: U.S.-Panamanian Relations, 1981–1990* (Boulder, CO: Lynne Reiner Publishers, 1991), 74–77.
41. Ropp, "National Security," 120–122.
42. For a description of these events, see Kevin Buckley, *Panama: The Whole Story* (New York, NY: Simon and Schuster, 1991), 80–101.
43. A detailed description of this and of other events leading up to the December US invasion (Operation *Just Cause*) are detailed in Lawrence A. Yates, *The U.S. Military Intervention in Panama: Origins, Planning and Crisis*

Management, June 1987–December 1989 (Washington, DC: Center for Military History, United States Army, 2008).

44. There are numerous journalistic accounts of Operation *Just Cause*. The most scholarly is edited by Bruce W. Watson and Peter G. Tsouras, *Operation Just Cause*. (Boulder, CO: Westview Press, 1991).

45. John T. Fishel, "The Institutional Reconversion of the Panamanian Defense Forces," in *Post-invasion Panama: The Challenges of Democratization in the New World Order*, ed. By Orlando J. Pérez (Lanham, MD: Lexington Books, 2000), 16–22.

46. Ibid., 18.

47. Margaret Scranton, "Consolidation and Imposition: Panama's 1992 Referendum," *Journal of Inter-American Studies and World Affairs*, Vol. 35, No. 3 (Fall 1993), 75–76.

48. Orlando J. Pérez, "Elites, Power and Ideology: The Struggle for Democracy in Panama," (Ph.D. dissertation, University of Pittsburgh, 1996), 240–241.

Chapter 5

Haiti: Prejudice and Poverty

The longest lasting, and, in many ways, most controversial of the American interventions was in Haiti, where the Marines essentially occupied the country from 1915 until 1934. Those years were marked by political controversy, racism, and periods of violent conflict. At the end, Haiti remained the Western Hemisphere's poorest nation with little prospects for escaping that position.

The product of slave rebellion, Haiti had long been viewed by many in the United States with a mixture of suspicion and contempt. Alone among the American Republics, it had French as its official language, but the vast majority of its population spoke Haitian Creole, a unique blend of several languages largely unknown in the rest of the world. While officially Catholic, the most practiced religion was *vodun* or voodoo, a syncretic mixture of African and Christian beliefs that further contributed to its isolation. Economics and politics were dominated by a small, French-speaking mulatto elite, concentrated in urban areas. It shared the island of Hispaniola with the Dominican Republic, but between these two nations there was a deep-rooted historical antipathy.

Haitian politics had always been violent, with few Presidents leaving office alive. It became easier and easier for aspirants to national power to recruit a force of unemployed peasants from the nation's north, provide them with rudimentary arms, and descend on the capitol of Port Au Prince, looting as they went. Known as *cacos,* most would then return to the north where they were available for the next would-be president. Some would join the national army which differed little from the *cacos* in armament, training, or discipline and which often had less motivation to fight.

Anxious to exclude European influences from Haiti, concerned over the safety of American investments and citizens, and at least mildly interested in acquiring a naval base, Washington had long sought to expand its influence. Efforts to establish a customs receivership repeatedly foundered on the twin rocks of Haitian intransigence and instability. By the beginning of 1915, President Woodrow Wilson was beginning to consider military intervention, something he wished to avoid.[1]

Events overtook policy. In July 1915, another *caco* army descended on Port Au Prince. Before fleeing to the French Legation, President Guillaume Sam had 161 political prisoners, many from elite families, murdered. An enraged mob broke into the legation and literally tore Sam apart.

An American Naval force, commanded by Rear Admiral William B. Caperton, had already been ordered to Haitian waters and, at the request of the diplomatic corps, quickly landed 330 Marines and armed sailors. There was no organized resistance, though two sailors were killed, allegedly by snipers, but most likely by other Americans.[2] The shooting spurred Caperton to disarm as many Haitians as possible, in the process ensuring that the task of policing Port Au Prince and eventually the entire nation would become the responsibility of the Marines.

Reinforcements for the initial landing party arrived steadily, but the ultimate goals of the intervention remained unclear. On 14 August, the Chief of Naval Operations wrote Assistant Secretary of the Navy, Franklin D. Roosevelt, "The State Department has not yet informed us of their exact policy in Haiti, but Mr. Lansing has expressed the intention of outlining an exact policy in the near future."[3]

Caperton could not wait for Washington to formulate a policy. On 3 September, he proclaimed Martial Law in "the territory now occupied by forces under my control," adding, "Military Authorities will not interfere in the functions of the Civil Administration and the Courts, except in so far as relates to person violating military orders or regulations or otherwise interfering with the exercise of Military Authority."[4]

A major issue quickly arose. The Haitian Congress was preparing to elect a new president and Washington wanted to insure it picked someone who would be amenable to its demands. There were two candidates, Rosalvo Bobo, leader of the most recent *caco* revolt and Senate President Philippe Sudré Dartiguenave. Navy Secretary Josephus Daniels cabled Caperton, "Allow election of President to take place whenever Haitians wish. The United States prefers election of Dartiguenave." Daniels later admitted, "this was equivalent to America making Dartiguenave President."[5] Caperton certainly saw it that way. He summoned Bobo and informed him that, "the United States forbids" his presidential candidacy.[6] The same message was transmitted to the Haitian Congress where, on 11 August 1915, with a squad of Marines inside the Chamber, Dartiguenave was elected President with 94 out of 116 votes.[7] He was immediately sworn into office.

Washington now had a Haitian President who appeared willing to accede to its demands. They were rapidly forthcoming. To insure Dartiguenave's cooperation, the Secretary of State sent him a personal message assuring him that America would "aid and protect you while you are administering Haitian Government provided you stand firm with the United States, no matter what course others may take," and adding that if his Cabinet should resign he should "form another Government of patriots which, in Haiti's interests, will accept wishes and guidance of the United States."[8]

Washington's immediate priority was obtaining a Treaty that would legitimize the occupation, establish firm control over finances, and provide for the development of a constabulary. As Secretary of State Lansing informed the American Chargé in Haiti: "It seems indispensible to organize and maintain a trained constabulary which will take the place of the Haitian Army and which, well-officered and properly equipped and disciplined will possess sufficient power to preserve order, suppress insurrections and protect life and property throughout the Republic."[9] Caperton didn't wait for a Treaty before beginning preparations for creating the constabulary. He seized control of Haiti's customs houses, then informed the American Legation that, "funds collected will be used for the organization and maintenance of an efficient constabulary."[10]

The Treaty was signed, following considerable American pressure, on 16 September 1915, but not finally ratified by the US Senate until February 1916. Its provision for the constabulary was the longest clause and provided:

> The Haitian Government obligates itself, for the preservation of domestic peace, the security of individual rights, and the observance of the provisions of this treaty, to create without delay an efficient constabulary, urban and rural, composed of native Haitians. This constabulary shall be organized and officered by Americans appointed by the President of Haiti upon nomination by the President of the United States. The Haitian Government shall clothe these officers with the proper and necessary authority and uphold them in the performance of their functions. These officers will be replaced by Haitians as they, on examination conducted under direction of a board to be selected by the senior American officer of this constabulary and in the presence of a representative of the Haitian Government, are found to be qualified to assume such duties. The constabulary herein provided for shall, under the direction of the Haitian government, have supervision and control of arms and ammunition, military supplies, and traffic therein throughout the country. The high contracting parties agree that the stipulations in this article are necessary to prevent factional strife and disturbances.[11]

Without waiting for ratification, the Marines immediately began putting the provisions of this article into practice. The most immediate issues were recruiting acceptable enlisted Haitians and procuring Marine officers. The latter proved somewhat simpler. The Marines made two decisions, both of which would serve as precedents for future constabulary development in the Dominican Republic and Nicaragua. The first was to draw most of the constabulary's junior officers from the ranks of the Marine's noncommissioned officers, mostly sergeants, but including some corporals. The second was that those commissioned in the new *Gendarmerie* (later designated as the *Garde d'Haiti*) would draw a salary from the Haitian government in addition to their regular pay. Since most Marines served at two or more ranks above their rank in the Corps this was a significant incentive and volunteers were not hard to find.[12]

Unfortunately, the Marines had little to go on, other than prior service records, when it came to selecting those detailed to the *Gendarmerie*. The potential pool was very limited and no Marine had significant experience in training and leading troops of a different race and culture and speaking a different language. The Marines also lacked experience in police duties as the Corps left this, along with medical services, to the Navy. Few Marine officers and almost no enlisted men were fluent in French, while none spoke Haitian Creole, the language of the population's vast majority. Most shared the racial prejudices of American society, which exposure to the appalling conditions of life in Haiti only strengthened.[13] These problems would get worse when many of the best qualified Marines were sent to Europe after America entered World War I.

Along with the development of the *Gendarmerie*, the Marines faced the necessity of disarming existing Haitian forces. In the case of the Army, this did not prove particularly difficult. Admiral Caperton preferred that this be done by paying for weapons and that succeeded with most of the old Haitian Army. Each man who turned in a rifle was paid fifteen *gourdes* (less than $3) and officers might get additional funds.[14] In some cases, existing municipal police were allowed to keep their weapons and remain on duty until the *Gendarmerie* could take their place. Dealing with the *cacos*, however, proved much more difficult. They were strongly opposed to the intervention, especially when Marines began to move into their traditional strongholds in the north. Caperton tried to negotiate payments with some of their leaders, but the results were disappointing. Ultimately, Marine patrols were sent into the countryside to forcibly disband them. After several sharp encounters, which produced few Marine but numerous *caco* casualties, resistance was broken and most of the surviving *cacos* disarmed.[15]

The *Gendarmerie* was not yet sufficiently organized to take part in these operations. In December 1915, Major Smedley Darlington Butler was appointed as that force's first commander with the Haitian rank of Major General. Butler had distinguished himself in the operations against the *cacos* and had the additional advantage of being the son of the Chairman of the House Naval Appropriations Committee. He was forceful, outspoken and ambitious. He was also strongly prejudiced against Haitians in general and the political leadership in particular. For example, he wrote Brigadier General John A. Lejeune:

> Things here in Haiti are at a standstill. This wretched Government absolutely refuses to sign any agreement which may deprive them of their graft. . . . I have told these miserable ministers what I think of them and if I stay here they know exactly what to expect. As far as I am able this country will be run as a piece of machinery, with no preference being shown any negro owing to a supposed superiority due to the infusement of white blood in his veins.[16]

A few months later he wrote, "This political situation here is becoming more ridiculous every day and in my opinion there is nothing to do, but kick the whole crowd out and have a military government."[17]

Despite his misgivings, Butler set out to recruit a force. This proved more difficult than had been anticipated. The lowest class of Haitians, some of who were forcibly conscripted, had always undertaken police and military duties. They rarely received much of their pay. Instead, their officers put the funds into their own pockets. It was difficult for them to conceive that conditions under the Marines would be any different. A requirement for minimal literacy was quickly dropped when it turned out that many recruits could not even speak French, much less read and write it. This meant that most training had to be done by the use of gestures and the exercise of physical force. In a few cases, Marines were able to procure the services of Jamaicans resident in Haiti who could speak both English and Creole. They received appointments as sergeants, but served largely as interpreters.[18] Health was also a problem. Medical examinations revealed that 95 percent of potential recruits had blood diseases and 85 percent were infected with worms.[19]

As a result, training had to be much more rudimentary and prolonged than initially envisioned. It was not until early February 1916 that any significant number of troops, referred to as *Gendarmes*, could be deployed outside of Port Au Prince. On 31 January 1916, Colonel Littleton Waller, the commander of the US Marines in Haiti, issued General Orders No. 35, detailing the duties of the force, then called the *Gendarmerie d'Haiti*. In addition to preserving order and protecting individuals and property, they were to control arms, prevent smuggling, take charge of roads, bridges, public building, telephone and telegraph services, irrigation services and public lands, collect vital statistics and make agricultural reports, undertake assorted health related activities including "preventing spread of animal diseases," control prisons, issue permits for internal travel, enforce weights and measures standard and enforce harbor and docking regulations.[20]

This huge list underscored the difficult tasks facing the new force. Their control over telephone and telegraph lines proved of short duration and was transferred to civil authorities, but most of the other functions continued to be exercised throughout the occupation. *Gendarmerie* detachments were often the only effective government presence in many rural areas giving them wide authority along with their extensive duties. Of course, how much attention was actually devoted to such tasks as controlling animal disease and supervising weights and measures is open to question.

General Orders No. 35 was amplified and placed on a firmer legal footing on 24 August 1916 with the signing of a Protocol between the United States and Haiti detailing the composition, duties, and authority of the *Gendarmerie*. This provided for a force of 116 officers and 2,533 enlisted men plus 16 clerks and a tiny coast guard of 44 officers and men. Pay ranged from $3,000 a year for the only general to $120 a year for privates. The total budget was $766,015 for the land forces and $35,048 for the coast guard. The protocol further stipulated that the force should "be considered the sole military and police force of the Republic of Haiti" and gave broad powers to its American commander.[21]

At the end of January, in an action which many Marines believed was designed to discredit the new force, but which more likely was adopted to consolidate presidential power, President Dartiguenave decreed the abolition of local law enforcement authority previously exercised by a variety of local officials with little central government control. This compelled Caperton to issue a hurried proclamation ordering that, "all the military and police duties heretofore performed by these officers be performed by the *Gendarmerie* of Haiti, supported by the expeditionary forces under my command."[22] Dispersing the *Gendarmerie* to posts throughout Haiti now became a matter of some urgency. Fortunately, this process proceeded relatively rapidly and smoothly. Most areas remained quiet, but there were numerous complaints of abuses of citizens and arbitrary arrests. The American Financial Advisor to Haiti admitted that:

The gendarmerie, which was in close contact with the peasants and villagers, had had an insufficient period of training and Haitian gendarmes, not yet thoroughly disciplined, exhibited that brutal disregard for individual rights which had been a habit with the police and soldiers of the old regime. It is probable too that some—though not many—of the American officers of the gendarmerie had the same attitude.[23]

Arming the Haitians presented a different set of problems. Originally they were given outdated weapons used by the old army, for which little reliable ammunition was available.[24] Some Marines, distrustful of black Haitians, opposed providing more modern weapons. But necessity ultimately prevailed and a quantity of Krag-Jorgensen rifles, the standard American weapon in the Philippines, were made available. This was none too soon as they were about to go into combat, joining the Marines in eliminating the remaining organized *cacos*. Earlier Marine successes had produced over 200 Haitian deaths, causing Navy Secretary Josephus Daniels to cable Caperton to curb his offensive operations and to "inform Department before taking steps that would lead to loss of life on either side except in cases of urgent necessity."[25] These restrictions, however, didn't necessarily apply to the constabulary. In any case, the effort to establish *Gendarme* posts in Haiti's north, the traditional *caco* stronghold produced numerous clashes in most of which the Haitian troops prevailed. There was, however, one especially embarrassing incident. While the Maine Sergeant/ *Gendarme* Lieutenant who commanded the prison in Port Au Prince was briefly absent, a massive jailbreak occurred. The escaping inmates, led by two *caco* chiefs, seized most of the prison guards' rifles and headed back north. Butler was convinced that at least some of the guards had connived in this, and was determined to help recapture the prisoners. As it turned out most were soon killed or captured by a mixed Marine-*Gendarme* patrol. One group of ten prisoners who had been captured allegedly tried again to escape and were all shot.[26] Despite the obviously suspicious nature of this account, no effort seems to have been made to investigate the killings or to discipline those responsible.

Relations between the *Gendarmerie* and the Haitian government were often difficult. This was in part due to Haitian efforts to maintain some degree of sovereignty, in part to Butler's personality and prejudices, and in part to disputes among Haitian political factions. President Dartiguenave was repeatedly caught between US pressures and nationalist sentiments, especially those of Haiti's Congress. His attempts to steer a middle course were constantly frustrated, both by Butler, who often treated him with disdain, and by the Congress which was determined to assert its independence.[27] All of these issues came to a head with Washington's determination to have Haiti adopt a new constitution which would be in line with the provisions of the Treaty and would also permit foreign land ownership. The latter had been prohibited since the expulsion of the French and the issue aroused strong nationalist antipathies. In an effort to deal with this, Dartiguenave had the *Gendarmerie* dissolve the Haitian Senate in April 1916. This action, however, also made impossible the adoption of a new constitution. In an effort to overcome this, both houses of the Haitian Congress were called into a combined session as a Constituent Assembly in early 1917. A draft constitution, at least partly written by then Assistant Secretary of the Navy Franklin D. Roosevelt (who later claimed authorship of the entire document) was presented to the Assembly that tried to ignore it. Instead there was an outburst of national feeling and a rush effort to push through a constitution distinctly at odds with Washington's desires. The assembly also refused an American request that it declare war on Germany.[28]

Both the United States and President Dartiguenave were increasingly concerned by the Assembly's independence. The president even feared it might attempt to impeach him. He and Butler agreed to its forcible dissolution. This was done on 19 June 1917, using what Butler described as "genuine Marine Corps methods."[29] With a squad of *gendarmes* he forced his way into the room where the Assembly was in session. When its president discovered his mission he began to bitterly attack the Americans and President Dartiguenave. According to Butler:

> The gendarmes, who had previously been Haitian soldiers and who had taken part in this dissolving function about every six months, had always been accustomed to shoot at this stage of the game, and when the President was criticized they all commenced to load their rifles, which created considerable confusion, and we had to suspend operations until we ran around and took the cartridges out of their guns. I was their chief and they were interested in my cause because I paid them and fed them and treated them squarely.[30]

He later described what happened next in an interview with Lowell Thomas:

> The hall was in an uproar. Tables and chairs were upset, deputies were surging forward. I had to calm down the

gendarmes who were clicking rifles again. Finally the presiding officer rang the dinner bell he used for a gavel and reluctantly read the presidential decree. He then declared the assembly dissolved and directed that the chamber be cleared. The gendarmes followed the unwilling legislators into the street and locked the door.[31]

Haiti would have no Congress for the next twelve years. Dartiguenave appointed a Council of State, but it had largely advisory powers. With considerable assistance from and pressure by the United States, notably Assistant Navy Secretary Franklin D. Roosevelt, a new Constitution was drafted. It included clauses making the *Gendarmerie* the "only armed force of the Republic," and allowing resident foreigners to own land. It also declared that, "All the acts of the United States during its military occupation of Haiti are ratified and validated."[32]

With the Assembly dissolved there was no legal way for the new Constitution to be ratified. Dartiguenave suggested that the document be submitted to a plebiscite. Washington, which recognized that this was of dubious legality and that asking an overwhelmingly illiterate population to vote on a lengthy legal document had obvious elements of farce, ultimately agreed. The plebiscite was held on 12 June 1918. *Gendarme* officers were charged with supervising the polls and distributing the ballots and were told to make sure the vote was favorable. They evidently had little difficulty accomplishing this since the final vote total was announced as 69,337 for and 335 against.[33] It is doubtful in many voters had any idea what they were voting for. One allegedly even thought he was electing a Pope. Not all American officials were comfortable with this result. After he became President, Roosevelt received a letter from Josephus Daniels, who, as Secretary of the Navy in 1918, had been his boss, saying:

> You know that the things we were forced to do in Haiti was a bitter pill for me . . . I never did wholly approve of that Constitution of Haiti you had a hand in framing . . . I expect in the light of experience we both regret the necessity of denying even a semblance of self determination in our control of Haiti when we had to go in and end revolutions or see some European government do so.[34]

While much of the *Gendarme* leadership was involved with national politics, and a few units were still engaging *cacos* in the north, most of the force settled down to more or less routine duties. As it became obvious that Caperton's original assurances that the occupation would be of short duration were not going to be fulfilled some Marine officers began bringing their wives and families to Haiti. This however, was not an option for those in rural areas that were isolated, impoverished, and generally inhospitable. Being assigned to such areas did have its advantages. As one observer noted:

> The marine who becomes an officer in the gendarmerie finds himself clothed with practically unlimited power in the district where he serves. He is the judge of practically all civil and criminal cases, settling everything from a family fight to a murder. He is paymaster for all funds expanded by the national government, he is ex-officio director of the schools, inasmuch as he pays the teachers. He controls the mayor and city council, since they can spend no funds without his o.k. As collector of taxes he exercises a strong influence on all individuals in the community.[35]

An extreme example of this authority was that exercised by Marine sergeant–*Gendarme* Lieutenant Faustin Wirkus, who had charge of the Haitian island of La Gonâve. Wirkus, who had already served in Haiti for several years before going to La Gonâve, made a sustained effort not only to learn Creole, but also to understand Haitian culture and religion. In the process he overcame most of his imported prejudices. He managed to so ingratiate himself on the island that, ultimately, at least some of the inhabitants, began addressing him as "the King."[36] American author William Seabrook, generally a critic of the intervention, wrote glowingly about Wirkus.[37] Cases like this, however, were the exception rather than the rule. Most officers carried out their duties efficiently, but had little if any social contact with local populations and largely failed to understand the culture. This was accentuated by frequent rotations of officers from post to post and by the relatively low educational level of the average enlisted Marine who was made a *Gendarme* junior officer.

One effort to incorporate what was believed to be a traditional part of Haitian life turned into a major disaster. This was the adoption of the *corvée*, the old French system of compulsory local labor on the roads. The French had built a considerable road network, but in the more than a century since they had been expelled these had fallen into disrepair. The Marines wanted an improved system to facilitate their operations and other Americans saw this as a key to efforts at economic development. But funds were scarce and, despite their poverty, almost no Haitians wanted to work on the roads. It was evidently Smedley Butler who discovered that there was an 1864 law still on the books that could compel local inhabitants who did not pay road taxes to work on them. As *Gendarme* Commander, most of the task of securing labor and building roads fell to his command and he undertook this with considerable enthusiasm. He had little trouble in selling this idea to his Marine Corps superiors. As General George Barnett, Commandant of the Corps from 1914 to 1920, later testified, "you can not have good military control, you can not have good business, you can not have good anything in a country without roads." Speaking specifically of Haiti, he then added, "The first thing that would occur to a military man, and did occur to them, was that before you could keep up any posts in the interior you had to have roads."[38]

At first the road construction projects seemed to go fairly well, especially the rebuilding of the road from Port Au Prince to Haiti's second city, Cape Haitien. Butler was enthusiastic, personally making one of the first trips on the road, but cautioned:

> It is not well to describe in a letter the methods we used to build this road, but it might be interesting to you to know that when this highway is finished, it will have cost the Haitian government only about $500 a mile. Since you were here we have opened nearly 400 miles of road in this country . . . We have over 15,000 at work in the whole of Haiti, a goodly sized body of intelligent voters for any project the United States may wish to put across. . . . Am taking His Excellency and his Cabinet to Cape Haitien and Ouanaminthe on January 5th for a big celebration and official opening of the road during which trip he will justify through his own people any rough stuff we may have employed in the building of the road.[39]

The "rough stuff" got worse the further the roads got from Port Au Prince. *Gendarme* officers were personally responsible for construction in areas under their jurisdiction and this led to abuses. The overall American military commander in the area, Rear Admiral H.S. Knapp, reported that in violation of the law Haitians had been compelled to work outside their home districts, and had been "marched to and from work bound together."[40] Local officials, who were charged with preparing lists of those eligible for roadwork, contributed to abuses, exercising favoritism extorting bribes, and making some individuals work repeatedly.[41]

Complaints mounted and the use of the *corvée* ultimately contributed to a revival of the *cacos*. Recognizing the problem, on 1 October 1918, the Marine Commander in Haiti ordered the system discontinued. One officer, however, Major Clarke H. Wells, Commander of the District of the North, historically the center of *caco* activity, ignored the order. In addition to continuing the *corvée*, with all its abuses, there were charges that Wells ordered his subordinates to kill prisoners and suppressed reports of these activities.[42] He was removed from his post, but never court-martialed for his offenses.

Resistance to the occupation broke out in late 1918 and within a few months achieved serious proportions. Charlemagne Péralte, who had been imprisoned by the Marines for earlier revolutionary activities, but had escaped, led the resistance. He turned out to be a natural and skillful insurgent commander. Within a few months, aided by the widespread discontent caused by the *corvée*, he had raised a force estimated at 5,000, supported by up to three times that number of part-time fighters and active sympathizers. He even developed an effective intelligence system, using Haitian market women to keep him informed of *Gendarme* and Marine movements.[43]

Major responsibility for dealing with this new outbreak devolved on the *Gendarmerie*, which had mixed success at best. Many of their officers were new in command and of a lesser quality than their predecessors, as many of the best men, including their first Commander, Smedley Butler, had been sent to Europe to fight in World War I.[44] Their dispersal in over a hundred small posts, combined with their lack of combat experience and outdated arms made it impossible for them to undertake an effective counter-insurgency campaign. That task increasingly fell to Marine unites, but they had seen their strength reduced due to World War I.

Charlemagne was finally killed by a covert *Gendarme* operation, involving two Marine non-commissioned officers holding *Gendarme* commission, plus a patrol of Haitian enlisted men. They were able, through an elaborate ruse, to penetrate his camp, kill him, and scatter his followers. For their exploits, the two Americans were awarded the Medal of Honor.[45] Charlemagne's death did not end the fighting, which dragged on into the spring of 1920. At one point, a *caco* force actually managed to break into Port Au Prince, but was soon driven off. A change in policy provided amnesty for those who surrendered and fighting wound down. When the last major *caco* commander was killed in 1920 the conflict essentially ended, although clashes with isolated groups, now largely criminal, continued for years. During the fighting the *Gendarmerie* lost five American officers and twenty-seven enlisted men killed while *caco* losses were estimated at 1,881 in 1919 and another 90 in early 1920.[46]

The problems with the *corvée* and the subsequent *caco* uprising had revealed serious deficiencies in the intervention's organization. Jurisdictions between the State Department, the Naval services, other Treaty officials, and the Haitian government were often confused and overlapping. While the State Department, at least in theory, had overall direction, its Minister in Haiti, Arthur Bailly-Blanchard was weak and often absent. The Navy Department generally deferred to the Admiral on the scene, but when the United States also occupied the neighboring Dominican Republic and Caperton's replacement, Rear Admiral H.S. Knapp, decided to makes his headquarters there, Naval direction suffered. The senior Marine officer in Haiti was the Brigade commander, but he had limited dealings with the Haitian government. The *Gendarmerie* Commander was always junior to him in rank. He was supposed to report to Haiti's president, but in reality usually looked for advice and support to the Brigade Commander. The Customs Receivership was nominally under the direction of the Army's Bureau of Insular Affairs, while the Financial Advisor reported to the State Department.[47] After 1917 all elements of the government in Washington were preoccupied with the war in Europe and gave little attention to Haitian affairs. When President Wilson was largely disabled by a stroke during his last seventeen months in office, coordination deteriorated still further. There seemed to be no clear direction or goals for the occupation, no concrete plans for Haiti's future.

The *Gendarmerie* suffered from this as well. When Colonel Frederic Wise returned to Haiti from Europe and took command of the force he found that conditions had deteriorated within the force and in its relations with the Marine Brigade. While units stationed in the capitol were in reasonably good shape, he found that rural units:

> ... were in bad shape. Their uniforms were in rags. Most of them were barefooted. Their rifles were a joke. They were discarded Krags, most of them with the sights knocked off. If they hit a house at point blank range with those weapons they were doing well. Their barracks were tumbledown. Their morale was pretty low. The Cacos seemed to have them bluffed.[48]

Wise also found credible accusations of the killing of prisoners and other abuses. He immediately set about trying to remedy these conditions, providing a determined leadership that the force had largely lacked since Butler's departure. Improvement in material conditions was steady. The troops were given new shoes and uniforms, armed with more modern Springfield rifles, and their quarters were repaired. The ration allowance was increased from ten to fifteen cents a day.[49] Troops began to get regular rifle training and soon demonstrated that they were very capable marksmen.

In 1924, a *Gendarmerie* rifle team tied with France for second place in the Olympic Rifle competition.[50]

The *Gendarmerie* also began to develop its own intelligence service. Previously, this had been a function of the Marine Brigade. During World War I, it had largely focused on the activities of those of German descent residing in Haiti, which might in part account for the failure to anticipate the *caco* uprising or to gauge the depth of resentment over the *corvée*.

The end of the *caco* uprising and the improved condition of the *Gendarmerie* meant that the remaining Marines could largely be concentrated in Port Au Prince and Cape Haitien and rural security left in *Gendarme* hands. From 1921 until 1929 the Marine Brigade saw almost no action and its strength at times dipped as low as five hundred.[51] American efforts to pacify Haiti seemed to have largely succeeded and the *Gendarmerie* was free to devote some of its attention to other matters such as a national immunization campaign when an outbreak of smallpox threatened.

The end of the *caco* revolt did not keep the occupation from becoming an issue in the 1920 US Presidential campaign, in part because Franklin D. Roosevelt was the Democrat's Vice-Presidential nominee. The Republican Presidential nominee and eventual victor, Senator Warren G. Harding, denounced the Democrat's policy in Haiti and declared, "I will not empower an Assistant Secretary of the Navy to draft a constitution for helpless neighbors in the West Indies and jam it down their throats by bayonets borne by United States Marines."[52]

In the fall of 1920, remarks such as this, combined with press accounts of abuses by the Marines and *Gendarmerie* caused the Navy Department to dispatch Admiral Henry T. Mayo to Haiti to head a Court of Inquiry. Both the Navy and the outgoing Wilson administration had an interest in sweeping abuses under the rug and the Court devoted most of its efforts to excusing the Marines. Only held three days of hearings were held in Haiti, during which it carefully avoided calling the *Gendarmerie* Commander, Colonel Frederic Wise, to testify.[53] The Court then issued its report that concluded:

> After a careful study of the matters in issue, based not only upon the evidence in the record, but also upon the court's own observations while in Haiti, the Court regards the charges which have been published as ill considered and thoroughly unwarranted reflections on a portion of the United States Marine Corps, which has performed difficult, dangerous, and delicate duty in Haiti in a manner

which, instead of calling for adverse criticism, is entitled to the highest commendation.[54]

The March 1921 inauguration of the Harding administration seemed to open the possibility of at least a thorough review if not a termination of the occupation. The purpose of continued occupation was certainly unclear. The original treaty had provided for US controls lasting for up to ten years with a possible extension for another ten years. In 1917, the United States and the Dartiguenave administration had hurriedly signed an agreement to extend the Treaty provisions until May 1936, but the Haitian Senate never ratified it. With that body dissolved, the legality of this agreement was open to question.[55] During the last months of the previous administration, civilian interest in and control over events in Haiti had been at low ebb and the Navy and Marines had been left to run things pretty much as they saw fit. Predictably, this meant an emphasis on maintaining order and avoiding controversy, with little attention paid to longer-range matters. An internal Marine Corps memorandum on the possibility of withdrawing the Brigade admitted that, "Haitians are, in general, opposed to the occupation and that a large majority of educated Haitians are opposed to the *Gendarmerie*." The author, however, justified the continuance of martial law and the use of Marine provost Courts to try Haitians on the grounds that Haitians feared them and if they were abolished it "would destroy all good accomplishments of occupation." If power were turned over to Haitians, "the time would truly be opportune for the Haitian politicians . . . to undermine the *Gendarmerie*." In conclusion, the author argued that, "it would be decidedly detrimental to the interests of both Haiti and the United States to withdraw the occupation, to abolish the existing martial laws or modified form of military government."[56] This essentially became the Marine position in discussions within the US government on the future of the occupation.

Despite election rhetoric, the Harding administration made no effort to end the occupation. It did, however, recognize the need for better control over events and coordination among the various agencies working in the country. The new Secretary of State, Charles Evans Hughes, had been asked by President Harding to recommend changes in US policy toward Haiti. Hughes responded by telling the President, "We cannot leave Haiti at the present time," and argued that the prime task should be to "perfect the methods of administration." This included efforts to improve the *Gendarmerie* and the appointment of a senior Marine officer as the President's personal representative to coordinate the work of all the American agencies in Haiti.[57]

In addition to Hughes' recommendations, the Harding administration had the recommendations of a lengthy Senate investigation of conditions in Haiti. A Committee of Inquiry, chaired by Senator Medill McCormick, was established in August 1921 to investigate the occupation of both Haiti and the Dominican Republic. McCormick made a much more serious effort then had Mayo and the lengthy report of his Committee included numerous recommendations for improving the administration of Haiti. But, in line with both State and Navy Department sentiment, it did not recommend terminating the occupation. Instead, it recommended that a High Commissioner be appointed to oversee and coordinate American policy. Hughes agreed and asked the Navy to recommend an active duty Marine officer for the post. Smedley Butler actively campaigned for the appointment, but the State Department feared he would rely on coercion instead of persuasion and asked the Navy to find someone else.[58] Colonel John H. Russell, who had commanded the Brigade in Haiti, was the next choice. He was quickly promoted to Brigadier General and appointed by President Harding as High Commissioner with the additional rank of Ambassador Extraordinary. His instructions came from Secretary of State Hughes who informed him:

> In the performance of your duties, you will be guided by instructions from the Secretary of State and will report to the Department of State on all matters other than those solely connected with the functions of the Commanding Officer of the United States Forces of Occupation. . . . All communications from the Government of the United States to the Government of Haiti will be conveyed to the Haitian Government through the High Commissioner. . . . It will be your duty to coordinate the work of the Treaty officials . . . and of the Commanding Officer of the United States Forces of Occupation in Haiti . . . and to bring about harmonious cooperation between these officials and the members of the Haitian Government.[59]

Hughes went on to say, "the history of our intervention in Haitian Affairs is not viewed with satisfaction by this Government," and to outline several areas the administration believed deserved priority attention. One of these was the *Gendarmerie*:

> It is understood that the United States Marines, composing the Forces of Occupation cannot be withdrawn from Haiti until the native constabulary, or gendarmerie, is better organized and disciplined than it is at present, without

a recurrence of disorder. Inasmuch as it is the desire of the Government of the United States to withdraw its Forces of Occupation as soon as it may be possible, it should be one of the chief purposes of your mission to assist the Haitian Government in improving the discipline and organization of the gendarmerie and in bringing about an increase in the number of men enlisted, if necessary, so as to make the gendarmerie, in as brief a period of time as possible, competent in itself to maintain order in Haiti without American assistance. It is believed that if such reorganization of the gendarmerie is taken up by the Haitian Government, with your support, the presence of the United States Forces of Occupation will not be necessary after a few years' time.[60]

Despite the tone of these instructions the United States was destined to continue its occupation for twelve more years.

Russell set out to fulfill his mandate immediately. One of the steps he took was to begin training Haitians to fill the junior officer ranks. At the outset of the occupation there had been some sentiment for rapidly training Haitian officers, but despite the protests of the Marine Brigade Commander, the Secretary of the Navy decided that all initial officers should be Marines.[61]

There were some early efforts to train Haitian officers. Ten French-speaking candidates recruited from the French-speaking mulatto elite were enrolled in an officer candidate class in 1915. All, however, soon left the program, in part because of cultural clashes, in part because some of their Marine instructors couldn't speak French, and in part because many of the Marines were prejudiced against the idea of Haitian officers.[62] *Gendarmerie* Commander, Smedley Butler, for example, wrote that:

> We have tried Haitian lieutenants, but have found them to be a failure by actual experience, and I believe that it will be necessary, for a time, to have all the officers of this force Americans. Under the leadership of our marines, the Constabularymen have put down disturbances in Haiti, showing that they will make very reliable, good policemen if officered by Americans.[63]

After Russell's appointment, the Marines began to appoint Haitians to the most junior officer posts. At first, there were only five Haitian officers in the entire force. These numbers were slowly augmented, largely by promotions from the ranks of the *Gendarmerie*. In addition, a revived *École Militaire* was established and admitted twelve students. Twelve more were later admitted to what was to be a two-year course of instruction.[64] By then end of 1925, the force had 53 Haitian officers, and by the end of 1928 a majority of the lieutenants and at least one captain were Haitians and half of the military sub-districts were totally manned by Haitian officers.[65]

The relative tranquility of much of the 1920s also made possible improved and expanded training of enlisted personnel. Recruits now underwent eight weeks of basic training before being sent to the field. In typical Marine fashion, this training included strong emphasis on marksmanship. There was also a program established to provide basic elementary education for enlisted men, most of who were illiterate when they joined. Health services were also expanded and the constabulary developed its own health service, including some Haitian physicians.[66] Secretary of State Charles Evans Hughes visited Haiti and reported, "The *Gendarmerie d'Haiti*, the local police force, has been most efficiently handled and brought to a very high standard of excellence. It has practically taken over the policing of the interior of Haiti and has made possible the withdrawal of the Marines."[67]

Other than the steady integration of Haitians into the junior ranks, the remainder of the 1920s passed with few major changes in the roles and missions of the constabulary. Perhaps most noteworthy was a November 1928 change in name from *Gendarmerie* to the *Garde d'Haiti*. The original name evidently arose from some confusion in the French translation of the Treaty and was seen as increasingly inappropriate given the military as well as police functions undertaken by the force. Some Marines complained, in part because no additional funds were appropriated to cover such costs as new stationery, but the new name became permanent.[68]

There was also some expansion of constabulary functions during this period. They took control of the Port Au Prince Fire Department. They built and maintained several small landing strips for airplanes throughout the Republic. Prisons came under their jurisdiction and while still far from ideal, in part because of inadequate Haitian Government funding, conditions were much better than during any previous period of Haitian history.

One area, which remained outside of the *Garde's* control, was national politics. The American control of the force in this area, as in many others, had its strengths and weakness. The strength was that in a nation where force had been the traditional arbiter of power the military/police were removed from the political equation. The weakness was that knowing they had no real influence over the *Garde*. Haiti's political leadership was essentially able to ignore it, often provide inadequate funding, and follow American dictates with little fear of a popular backlash. Haitian presidents, along with some of the Marines, repeatedly tried to use the constabulary to harass and arrest opposition figures, especially those of the press. This raised concerns in Washington which feared the results of turning critics into martyrs and became a major source of contention between the Haitian Government and the State Department.[69]

Elections, or the lack thereof, also became a growing source of discontent. President Dartiguenave had wanted to succeed himself in 1922, but the United States vetoed that idea. Not wanting popular elections, Washington, and those Haitians anxious to cooperate with its desires, managed to have the appointed Council of State select Louis Borno as president for the next six-year term. No Congress or local officials were elected. The United States imposed Constitution stipulated that Congressional elections should be held every two years unless the President stipulated that conditions would not allow this. Borno so stipulated in both 1924 and 1926. He also had his handpicked Council of State elect him to a second term in 1926. When this seemed to arouse little popular protest he decreed that there would be no election in 1928. In agreement with Russell, Borno also had several Constitutional Amendments, including one extending his term until 1930, submitted to a plebiscite despite the absence of any Constitutional grounds for such a procedure. Once again the plebiscite was a farce, with the Government announcing that the amendments had been approved by a vote of 177,436 to 3,799.[70] By this time, the process was becoming a growing source of discontent within Haiti and of potential embarrassment in Washington. When the world depression hit Haiti the following year the stage was set for major confrontations.

On 5 October 1929, with the reluctant acquiescence of the State Department, Borno announced that there would be no elections in 1930 and that the Council of State would once again choose a President. Dana Gardner Munro, who as a senior State Department official supported this decision, later admitted, "In the light of hindsight, the wisdom of this decision seems doubtful. The consequences of holding an election might have been less embarrassing to the United States than what did happen."[71]

What did happen was a wave of popular protests. They began with strikes by students at the Central Agricultural School, but quickly spread. Borno wanted the protests crushed and opposition political leaders arrested, but Russell, at first, refused. As government workers began to join the strike, both Russell and Borno began to fear that the *Garde's* loyalty might not be reliable. While these fears ultimately proved illusory, a nervous Russell declared a state of martial law, something that had originally been decreed in 1915 and never officially revoked, and asked for Marine reinforcements.[72]

Despite continued anti-American and anti-Borno demonstrations, the situation seemed under control when, on 6 December, a Marine patrol fired on demonstrators in the coastal town of Aux Cayes, killing at least twelve and wounding a least 23 others.[73] Promptly dubbed the "Aux Cayes Massacre" this event doomed the Russell-Borno regime and set the stage for ending the occupation.

President Herbert Hoover had expressed concern over events in Haiti in his 3 December 1929 State of the Union message. Noting the presence of Marines in Haiti, Nicaragua, and China he had declared, "we do not wish to be represented abroad in such a manner." Referring directly to Haiti, which he characterized as a "difficult problem, the solution to which is still obscure," he announced his plan to "send a commission to Haiti to review and study the matter in an endeavor to arrive at some more definite policy than at present."[74]

Following the events at Aux Cayes, the promised commission was hurriedly established. Headed by W. Cameron Forbes and therefore known as the Forbes Commission, it arrived in Haiti on 28 February 1930 and stayed until 16 March. While there it not only prepared a report for the President, it forged a political agreement between Borno and his opponents which led to the selection of Eugene Roy as provisional President, serving from May until November 1930. Legislative elections were to be held in October and the new Haitian Congress would then choose a President to take office in November.[75] Elections were held on schedule, resulting in an overwhelming victory for the opponents of Borno and the critics of the U.S. occupation. The new Congress then chose one of the most prominent critics, Sténio Vincent, as President for a six-year term.[76]

While in Haiti, the Forbes Commission looked into most aspects of the occupation, including the *Garde*. The American commander of that force, Major General Frank E. Evans, told the Commissioners that, "The need for an efficient Haitian *Garde* is clear," and that Haitian officers wanted "some form of legislation that would protect them from displacement by any political favorite." After criticizing the Haitian political class he concluded that Haiti's future depended on "an efficient *Garde* and the legislation needed to insure its permanency and freedom from political influence."[77]

Some of the Commissioners were worried that the *Garde*, itself, might become an instrument of repression once the Marines departed, but their

66

greatest concern was the slow pace of Haitianization of the force.[78] By the time they arrived, only 2 of the *Garde's* 23 captains, 17 of 58 first lieutenants, and 17 of its 57 second lieutenants were Haitians. In addition, there were 28 Haitian cadet officers.[79] The Commission strongly recommended the adoption of the plan for Haitianization that it had drawn up and its relatively speedy enactment.[80]

The Commissions Report and the replacement of Borno, first by Roy and then by Vincent, insured the end of Russell's tenure as High Commissioner. He left Haiti and the office was abolished. The State Department was determined to regain control over Haitian affairs and named Dana Gardner Munro as Minister to Haiti, filling a post that had been vacant since Russell had been made High Commissioner. The Marines and the Navy Department, which had dominated Haitian affairs for the previous dozen years, were now clearly in a subordinate position.[81]

One of the first steps taken to Haitianize the *Garde* was to establish a permanent *École Militaire* with regulations modeled on those of that of the US Naval Academy. The course, however, lasted only a year.[82] Classes were regularly graduated every year from 1931 through 1934, providing sufficient officers to man the *Garde.*

The process of Haitianization was steady, but not always smooth. Vincent proved more difficult to deal with than Borno and there were repeated efforts to exert political influence over the *Garde.* One such dispute involved Vincent's refusal to approve the promotion of a Haitian lieutenant to captain on the grounds that he had made "disparaging remarks." The State Department was willing to give in on the issue, but Munro pressed the point, arguing that to give in would set a dangerous precedent of political control over *Garde* promotions and ultimately Vincent relented.[83]

This did not end the Haitian Governments efforts at exerting political influence. In September 1931, Vincent's Minister of the Interior wrote to the *Garde* Commander, ordering him to issue instructions that the *Garde's* police must obey all his requests. This contradicted the existing principle that all orders had to be given through the Commander and he refused to comply.[84]

Despite such conflicts, the Haitianization process continued. In late 1930, the first Haitian was promoted to major and placed in command of one of Haiti's departments. Two more promotions and subsequent appointments to department commands followed in 1932. By early 1934 a Haitian officer was in command in all the districts. This was not fast enough for the Vincent administration that wanted the process speeded up. General R.P. Williams, the Marine Commander of the *Garde,* defended the progress, noting that, as of November 1931, 109 of the 195 officers were now Haitians and the remaining slots would be filled as more classes graduated from the *École Militaire.* He added that early in 1932 a Haitian major would be promoted to colonel and two others would be promoted to major. He pointed out that Haitians were being promoted faster than their Marine counterparts and that the process of Haitianizaton was running well ahead of that projected by the Forbes Commission.[85]

The impact of the Depression complicated the process. The Vincent administration tried to reduce the budget for the *Garde,* and demanded a major reduction in the allowances given to Marines who served with it. How much of this was the result of actual budgetary pressure and how much was a political maneuver to gain increased control is impossible to determine since both factors were clearly present. In any case, after consultations between the State and Navy Departments, the United States agreed to a 15 percent reduction in the allowances given to Marines, but continued to press for full funding of the *Garde.*[86] Haiti briefly considered asking for an American Military Mission to be sent to continue training the *Garde* after the occupation ended, but ultimately did not pursue the idea.

The final US withdrawal, originally planned for 1936, was moved up to 1934, with Assistant Secretary of State Francis White telling Munro in 1931 that the President wanted "to withdraw from Haiti immediately if that were possible."[87] If anything, the victory of Democratic candidate Franklin D. Roosevelt in the 1933 elections may have speeded up the process. There were some final minor disputes over transferring title of equipment and property that legally belonged to the Marines to *Garde* and the United States eventually simply donated much of this. Training programs were set up to prepare Haitian officers for assuming total command and other programs were established for those who would assume duties as quartermasters and medical directors. On 1 August 1934, Colonel Demosthenes Calixte, who had originally enlisted in the *Garde* as a private, took command and two weeks later the last Marine unit left Haiti.[88] Although the United States retained some control over Haitian finances until 1947, the occupation was over.

The United States had created Haiti's first truly professional armed force. In the process, it had virtually ended the banditry and disorder which had long plagued the countryside, had broken the power of local strongmen and eliminated much of the graft and corruption which had always characterized local politics, and had forever ended the danger of governments being overthrown by *caco* or other irregular armies recruited by disaffected political leaders. What had not been done, of course, was to change the basic political culture where a small, ambitious elite dominated a largely illiterate and impoverished population. With politics circumscribed by Washington and the *Garde* controlled by the Marines, there was no viable pattern of civil-military relations, no formal instruments of civilian control, and little trust and/or communication between the political class and the officer corps. This situation would play out with generally disastrous results in Haiti's future.

Problems between Vincent and the *Garde* increased following the Marines departure. Anger over the Government's failure to respond to a massacre of Haitian peasants in the Dominican Republic led to an abortive plot by a group of officers in 1937. It was discovered and Colonel Calixte was ousted as *Garde* Commander and sent into exile.[89] Vincent then purged the officer corps of all those whose loyalty was suspect.[90]

Washington was able to block Vincent's desire to perpetuate himself in office and Élie Lescot became President in 1941. He promptly declared himself "Commander in Chief of the Armed Forces." After Pearl Harbor, Haiti quickly declared war on the Axis and, in return, received a large supply of equipment and some US training for the *Garde* which acquired artillery, tanks and aircraft.[91] Lescot used the war as an excuse to repress political opposition and extend his control over the *Garde*. An abortive 1945 plot against the President by some enlisted men was discovered and seven alleged ringleaders were summarily executed.[92]

In 1946, when Vincent tried to extend his time in office, student riots broke out and the *Garde's* officers forced him to resign. This coup, the first but not the last made by the *Garde*, established a military junta that also dismissed the Congress. They promised to hold new elections and to turn over power to whatever civilian government was selected.[93] To the surprise of many, this is exactly what happened. Dumarsais Estimé became President before the end of 1946 and the following year he renamed the *Garde* the *Armee d'Haiti*.[94]

The change in title did not produce a change in behavior. In 1950, the military again intervened, ousted Estimé and, following a questionable election, installed its own Commander, Colonel Paul Magloire, as president. Six years later the military forced him out. Elections the following year were won by Dr. François Duvalier, popularly known as "Papa Doc." He soon established the most tyrannical and prolonged rule in modern Haitian history.

Surprisingly, one of the new President's first acts was to ask for an American military mission to undertake the training of the military. He specifically wanted a Marine mission. The United States had established missions in most Latin American nations, but they were under Army, not Marine, control. His requests became more urgent when a strange conglomeration of former Haitian officers and Dade County deputy sheriffs tried to invade Haiti and overthrow him. This predictably failed, but the following year, with the ascension of Fidel Castro to power in Cuba, US concerns over Haitian security grew. Another abortive invasion, this time including Cubans as well as Haitians, heightened anxieties in Haiti and in Washington.[95] A mission, led by Marine Colonel Robert Debs Heinl, was dispatched in January 1959. It almost immediately began to find itself in conflict with the regime.

Papa Doc never trusted the military. He saw the US mission as a means of keeping them out of politics while at the same time strengthening their ability to defeat efforts to overthrow him. But, at the same time, he created a force of armed political thugs, known as the *Tonton Macoutes*, or the Volunteers in National Service, as a politically reliable counterweight to the military. As Duvalier repression grew, his problems with Washington and with his own military increased and there were several aborted attempts to overthrow him. All of this placed the Marine mission in an impossible position, but they stayed on until March 1963 when the failure of an attempt to get the Dominican military to help oust Duvalier made their position impossible.[96]

Despite continued efforts to overthrow him Papa Doc clung to power until his death in 1971. The Presidency was inherited by his son, Jean-Claude Duvalier, known as "Baby Doc." While not as conspicuously brutal as his father he may have been, he was even more corrupt. In February 1986, a combination of widespread anti-regime riots and demonstrations and US pressures convinced Baby Doc to go into exile. A military junta took over.[97]

The next few years were chaotic. In 1990 a charismatic but somewhat unstable ex-priest, Jean-Bertrand Aristide, was elected President. His policies rapidly collided with the interests of the military and he was overthrown and sent into exile. The United States refused to recognize the new regime, headed by General Raoul Cédras and pushed for the restoration of Aristide. This led to a US military intervention in 1994. Although there was no actual fighting, one result of this was the total destruction of the Haitian military. The force that Washington had created it had now helped destroy.[98]

Notes

1. For a detailed description of Wilson administration efforts to deal with Haiti without military intervention, see Dana Gardner Munro, *Intervention and Dollar Diplomacy in the Caribbean, 1900–1921* (Santa Barbara, CA: Greenwood Press Reprint, 1980), 329–351.

2. Anne Cipriano Venzon, ed., "Smedley D. Butler to Maud. D. Butler, August 1, 1915," *General Smedley Darlington Butler: The Letters of a Leatherneck, 1898–1931* (New York, NY: Praeger, 1992), 153.

3. Admiral Benson to Franklin D. Roosevelt, 14 August 1915, Franklin D. Roosevelt Papers, Naval Affairs, Box 12, Franklin Delano Roosevelt Presidential Library, Hyde Park, NY.

4. W.B. Caperton, "Proclamation to the People of Port Au Prince, Haiti," 3 September 1915, Papers of Smedley Darlington Butler, Marine Corps Historical Archives, Quantico, VA.

5. Hans Schmidt, *The United States Occupation of Haiti, 1915–1934* (New Brunswick, NJ: Rutgers University Press, 1971), 73.

6. Captain E.L. Beach, "Admiral Caperton in Haiti," National Archives and Record Service, Naval Records Collection of the Office of Naval Records and Library, RG 45, Subject File, Box 850.

7. David Healy, *Gunboat Diplomacy in the Wilson Era: The United States Navy in Haiti, 1915–1916* (Madison, WI: The University of Wisconsin Press, 1976), 113.

8. Quoted in cable from Franklin D. Roosevelt, Acting Secretary of the Navy, to Flag, USS *Washington*, 25 August 1915, National Archives and Record Service, Naval Records Collection of the Office of Naval Records and Library, RG 45, Subject File, Box 632.

9. The Secretary of State to Chargé Davis, 22 August 1915, full text included in Arthur C. Millspaugh, *Haiti Under American Control* (Boston, MA: World Peace Foundation, 1931), 208–209.

10. Admiral Caperton to US Chargé in Haiti, 2 September 1915, National Archives and Record Service, Naval Records Collection of the Office of Naval Records and Library, RG 45, Tray 47.

11. Treaty Between the United States and Haiti, Finances, Economic Development and Tranquility of Haiti, Signed at Port Au Prince, 16 September 1915, full text included in Millspaugh, 211–215.

12. For details of the extra pay and rank structure, see Schmidt, 88–89.

13. For details on the impact of this prejudice, see Schmidt, 79–81.

14. Healy, 159–160. For a description of one Marine's experience, see Colonel Frederic M. Wise and Meigs O. Frost, *A Marine Tells It to You* (New York, NY: J.H. Sears and Co., 1929), 132–133.

15. Edward Bimberg Jr., "Black Bandits of Haiti," *Leatherneck* (August 1941), 6–9; Smedley Butler to Thomas Butler, 5 October 1915, *General Smedley Darlington Butler*, 154–157.

16. Butler to Lejeune, 13 July 1916, Papers of General John A. Lejeune, Box

4, Marine Corps Historical Archives, Quantico, VA.

17. Butler to Lejeune, 22 June 1917, Papers of General John A. Lejeune, Box 4, Marine Corps Historical Archives, Quantico, VA.

18. Lieutenant General Julian C. Smith, USMC (Retired), Interview by author, Arlington, VA, April 1966.

19. Schmidt, 86–87; James H. McCrocklin, compiler, *Garde D'Haiti, 1915–1934: Twenty Years of Organization and Training by the United States Marine Corps* (Annapolis, MD: The United States Naval Institute, 1956), 60–62. McCrocklin was listed as compiler after it was discovered that much of the volume had been taken almost verbatim from the Marine Corps' own Final Report written by future General Franklin A. Hart.

20. Gendarmerie d'Haiti, General Orders Number 35, 31 January 1916, Papers of Smedley Darlington Butler, Marine Corps Historical Archives, Quantico, VA.

21. "Protocol Carrying Out the Provisions of Art. X of the Treaty of September 6, 1915, with Reference to the Formation of a Gendarmarie and its Command, Signed at Washington August 24, 1916," text in Millspaugh, 217–220.

22. Quoted in Harry Thomas Hance, "Civil-Military Relations: The Organization and Control of the Constabulary Force of the Republic of Haiti, 1915–1934" (M.A. thesis, The Ohio State University, 1965), 25.

23. Millspaugh, 88.

24. McCrocklin, 63.

25. Daniels to Caperton, 20 November 1915, quoted in Healy, 183.

26. Butler to Ethel C.P. Butler, 4 June 1916, in *General Smedley Darlington Butler*, 177–181.

27. For an example of the problems between Butler and Dartiguenave, see Butler to Ethel C.P. Butler, 18 July 1916, *General Smedley Darlington Butler*, 186–187.

28. Millspaugh, 74.

29. Butler to John A. McIlhenny, 23 June 1917, *General Smedley Darlington Butler*, 194–195.

30. Testimony of Smedley D. Butler, before the US Congress, Senate, Select Committee on Haiti and Santo Domingo, *Inquiry Into Occupation and Administration of Haiti and Santo Domingo*, Senate Report, 67th Congress, 1st and 2nd sessions, 1922.

31. Lowell Thomas, *Old Gimlet Eye: The Adventures of Smedley D. Butler as Told to Lowell Thomas* (New York, NY: Farrar and Reinhart, 1933), 216.

32. A copy of key clauses of this constitution are included in Millspaugh, 222–225.

33. Millspaugh, 76. It is doubtful if many of the voters had any idea what they were voting for.

34. Josephus Daniels to Roosevelt, 15 July 1933, quoted in E. David Cronon, *Josephus Daniels in Mexico* (Madison, WI: The University of Wisconsin Press, 1960), 68.

35. Samuel Guy Inman, quoted in Schmidt, 90.

36. Faustin Wirkus and Taney Dudley, *The White King of La Gonâve* (Garden City, NY: Doubleday, Doran and Co., 1931).

37. William Seabrook, "Introduction," in Wirkus and Dudley, xi–xv.

38. "Testimony of Major General George Barnett," US Senate, *Inquiry*, 488.

39. Butler to McIlhenny, 31 December 1917, Papers of Smedley Darlington Butler, Marine Corps Historical Archives, Quantico, VA.

40. Admiral H.S. Knapp to Navy Secretary Josephus Daniels, 2 November 1920, quoted in Schmidt, 101.

41. Hance, 54.

42. Schmidt, 104–105.

43. McCrocklin, 103–105.

44. Most career Marines wanted to be assigned to European Service. In addition, heavy casualties in such actions as Belleau Wood, made finding experienced replacements a matter of some urgency.

45. McCrockllin, 113–119.

46. Ibid., 125.

47. Millspaugh, 64–70.

48. Wise and Frost, 308–309.

49. Ibid., 309–310.

50. McCrocklin, 165–167.

51. Richard L. Millett and G. Dale Gaddy, "Administering the Protectorates: The U.S. Occupation of Haiti and the Dominican Republic," *Revista/Review Interamericana*, Vol. VI, No. 3 (Fall, 1976), 391.

52. Quoted in Hance, 75.

53. Wise later wrote that he had warned the Board not to call him as a witness because "if they put me on the stand under oath I was going to tell the truth." Wise and Frost, 334.

54. Quoted in Hance, 76.

55. Emily Green Balch, ed., *Occupied Haiti: Being the Report of a Committee of Six disinterested Americans, representing organizations exclusively American, who, having personally studied conditions in Haiti in 1926, favor the restoration of the Independence of the Negro Republic* (New York, NY: The Writers Publishing Company, 1927), 23.

56. "Memorandum Concerning the Replacing of the Present Occupation of Haiti with a Legation Guard," 1919, USMC–Haiti, Tray 228, RG 127, Records of the United States Marine Corps, National Archives.

57. Hughes to Harding, 19 July 1921, quoted in Dana Gardner Munro, *The United States and the Caribbean Republics, 1921–1933* (Princeton, NJ: Princeton University Press, 1974), 77.

58. Munro, *The United States and the Caribbean Republics*, 84. Munro was a senior official in the State Department's Latin American Division and reportedly led the move to reject Butler.

59. Hughes to Brigadier General John H. Russell, 11 February 1922, The Papers of Warren G. Harding, Box 182, Ohio State Historical Archives, Columbus, Ohio.

60. Hughes to Russell, The Papers of Warren G. Harding, 11 February 1922, Box 182, Harding Papers.

61. Colonel Littleton Waller to Lejeune, 10 October 1915, Papers of General John A. Lejeune, Box 4, Marine Corps Historical Archives, Quantico, VA.

62. McCrocklin, 92.

63. Butler to Mr. Mann, 4 April 1916, Papers of Smedley Darlington Butler, Marine Corps Historical Archives, Quantico, VA.

64. McCrocklin, 145–146.

65. Millspaugh, 112.

66. McCrocklin, 147–48, 157, 162–63.

67. Hughes to Harding, 16 June 1923, The Papers of Warren G. Harding, Box 182.

68. Hance, 81–82.

69. Munro, *The United States and the Caribbean Republics*, 110–111.

70. Schmidt, 192–193.

71. Munro, *The United States and the Caribbean Republics*, 311.

72. Ibid., 312.

73. Schmidt, 200. The Haitian press claimed 24 killed and 51 wounded.

74. President Herbert Hoover, "State of the Union Message," 3 December 1929, www.let.rug.nl/usa/P/hh31/speeches/hh_1929.htm.

75. For details of these developments see Robert M. Spector, *W. Cameron Forbes and the Hoover Commissions to Haiti (1930)* (Lanham, NY: University Press of America, 1985), 73–101.

76. Schmidt, 219.

77. Quoted in Spector, 134–135.

78. The use of the term "Haitianization" seems to have begun about this time. It has odd echoes of the program of Vietnamization that would be proclaimed over 40 years later.

79. Spector, 136.

80. "Report of the Forbes Commission," *Papers Relating to Foreign Relations of the United States,* Vol. III (Washington, DC: Government Printing Office, 1930), 227.

81. The Navy Department did attempt, with some success, to curb the Minister's authority over the Marine Brigade, but had to agree to limit Brigade relations with the Haitian Government "to such matters as may be agreed on with the Minister." Navy Secretary Adams to Secretary of State Stimson, 3 February 1931, National Archives and Record Service, Records of the United States Department of State, RG 59, 838.00/2929 1/2.

82. Michael S. Laguerre, *The Military and Society in Haiti* (Knoxville, TN: University of Tennessee Press, 1993), 77; McCrocklin, 208–210.

83. There are numerous messages between Munro and the Department on this issue printed in *Papers Relating to Foreign Relations of the United States*, Vol. II (Washington, DC: Government Printing Office, 1931), 475–481; see also Munro, *The United States and the Caribbean Republics*, 328–329.

84. Hance, 96.

85. General R.P. Williams to Munro, 20 November 1931, RG 127, Tray 38.

86. Memorandum of phonecall by the Assistant Secretary of State to the Assistant Secretary of the Navy, 29 June 1933, RG 59, 838.00/3149.

87. White to Munro, 5 March 1931, quoted in Schmidt, 222.

88. Hance, 96.

89. Laguerre, 85–86; D.P. Calixte, *Haiti: Calvary of a Soldier* (New York, NY: Wendell, Malliet & Co., 1939), 71–86.

90. Richard A. Hagerty, ed., *Haiti: A Country Study* (Washington, DC: Government Printing Office, 1989), 16.

91. Charles T. Williamson, *The U.S. Naval Mission to Haiti, 1959–1965* (Annapolis, MD: Naval Institute Press, 1999), 8.

92. Robert D. and Nancy G. Heinl, *Written in Blood: The Story of the Haitian People, 1492–1971* (Boston, MA: Houghton Mifflin, 1978), 543.

93. Laguerre, 91–93.

94. Hagerty, 16.

95. James Ferguson, *Papa Doc, Baby Doc: Haiti and the Duvaliers* (Oxford, UK: Basil Blackwell, 1987), 41–42.

96. Williamson's book is a fascinating and detailed account of the travails of this mission and the nature of the Duvalier regime. The conflict with the Dominican Republic is detailed in John Bartlow Martin, *Overtaken by Events* (Garden City, NY: Doubleday and Co., 1966), 416–417.

97. Ferguson, 112–121.

98. For a description of this period, see Walter E. Kretchik, Robert F. Baumann, and John T. Fishel, *Invasion, Intervention, "Intervasion:" A Concise History of the U.S. Army in Operation Uphold Democracy* (Fort Leavenworth, KS: US Army Command and General Staff College Press, 1998).

Chapter 6

Dominican Republic: An Unintended Foundation for Tyranny

The Dominican Republic shares the island of Hispaniola with Haiti and has over sixty percent of the land including the most fertile areas and the best beaches. As a nation it had to gain independence twice, first from Spain and then from an occupation by Haiti. This began the traditional, deep-seated animosity between the two nations. Its strategic position, athwart the Windward Passage, long made it an object of international interest especially on the part of the United States. During the Grant administration, an effort was made to annex the nation, then known as Santo Domingo. A treaty was negotiated and the American flag raised, but ratification failed in the Senate by a single vote.[1]

Dominican politics were factionalized along family and regional rather than ideological lines and force. Votes were not the traditional arbiter. One result was a rising national debt, much of it owed to European creditors. During Theodore Roosevelt's administration, the United States got directly involved. The State Department began efforts to negotiate a Treaty which would establish an American Customs Receivership, would give Washington the option of leasing a naval station at Samana Bay, something much of the Navy ardently desired, and which might even include the right of military intervention to restore order. The President, at first, was reluctant to pursue the issue, writing a friend:

> I want to do nothing, but what a policeman has to do in Santo Domingo. As for annexing the island, I have about the same desire to annex it as a gorged boa constrictor might have to swallow a porcupine wrong-end-to. . . . If I possibly can, I want to do nothing to them. If it is absolutely necessary to do something, then I want to do as little as possible.[2]

The continued problem of Dominican debts to Europe, coupled with the possibility that this might produce European intervention ultimately changed the President's mind. In January 1905, a Treaty was signed establishing an American customs receivership, but it ran into trouble gaining Senate ratification. Roosevelt tried to justify the Treaty in his 5 December 1905 State of the Union Address, declaring, "there was imminent danger of foreign intervention," and adding, "at least two foreign nations were on the point of intervening and were only prevented from intervening by the unofficial assurances of this government that it would itself strive to help Santo Domingo."[3]

The 1905 Treaty was never ratified, but a Customs Receivership was established under a *modus vivendi*. A slightly revised Treaty was negotiated in 1907 and this time received prompt Senate ratification, but was held up for several months before finally being ratified by the Dominican Congress.[4] This ended any threat of European intervention, but failed to stabilize the Republic's internal politics.

Political struggles revolved around the long-standing rivalry between the followers of General Horacio Vázquez and the partisans of ex-President Isidro Jiménez. By the second decade of the 20th century a third faction, loyal to regional strongman Desiderio Arias emerged, adding to the conflict. A suggestion by the American Minister that promoting baseball might offer "a real alternative to the excitement of revolutions," was of little help and in 1914, only the threat of US intervention caused all parties to agree to Washington's demand that they select a provisional President, hold elections, and abide by the results.[5]

Regional uprisings broke out again in 1915. The United States, which had just occupied neighboring Haiti, was in no mood to tolerate renewed conflict and William Russell, the American Minister, demanded that the Republic cease increasing its debt, accept an American financial advisor and permit the United States to create a constabulary, replacing existing military and police forces.[6] The government and its opponents joined in rejecting these demands, but Washington was now just waiting for an excuse to impose them.

That excuse was not long in coming. In April 1916, Desiderio Arias occupied the capital and forced Congress to impeach President Isidro Jiménez. Jiménez began gathering his own army to attempt to oust Arias. Russell pressured Jiménez to ask for American intervention against Arias, but instead Jiménez suddenly resigned. Russell then confronted Arias with the demand that he surrender or be attacked by the Marines who had already begun landing.[7] Arias refused, but fled the capital and the Marines quickly occupied the city without resistance. Admiral William B. Caperton, who was also in command of the American occupation of Haiti, seemed unsure as to what to do next. When he asked the Navy Department what American policy was, the reply directed him to "consult with the American Minister, examine the archives of the legation, and obtain therefrom the policy of the United States."[8]

More Marines were landed and some sent north where they rapidly compelled the surrender of the forces loyal to Arias. But, in the capital, events were not going as well. The Dominican Congress met to elect a new president and Minister Russell tried to use the threat of force to secure a candidate favored by the United States. American control, however, was not nearly as complete as in Haiti and the Dominicans were not nearly as compliant as their Haitian counterparts. Russell's effort to arrest some senators only further inflamed Dominican nationalism and they elected a candidate who refused to give prior assurance of complying with US demands for greater financial controls and creating an American-led constabulary.[9] As a result, Washington refused to recognize the new government and the customs receiver cut off all its funds.

This stalemate continued until November. With economic conditions deteriorating, new elections pending, and the government still unwilling to concede to all of Washington's demands, a conference between State and Navy officials determined to declare martial law and install a Military Government. They argued that, "in order to legalize our action in keeping order and putting down any revolutionary activity it is considered that the only remedy will be the declaration of martial law."[10] Navy Captain Harry Knapp, who had succeeded Caperton as area Commander, drafted a proclamation that Wilson reluctantly approved and, on 29 November 1916, Knapp proclaimed a full military occupation with himself as Governor. Most Dominican officials would be allowed to remain in their posts, but would operate "under the oversight and control of United States Forces exercising Military Government."[11]

It was originally intended that the Military Government be of relatively short duration, but this was not to be the case. The bulk of Dominican officials refused to serve under the American authorities. On 8 December, Knapp declared all cabinet offices vacant and appointed Navy and Marine officers to fill them. Secretary of the Navy Josephus Daniels disapproved this action, causing Knapp to complain that reversing his position caused "loss of prestige and embarrassment to the Military Government." Explaining that he could not order Dominicans to fill the posts and that his action would only be temporary, he concluded, "The Military Government will be saved much embarrassment if by Sunday night I receive an approval of my action." At this point Daniels gave in with the proviso that US officials could assume the duties but not the titles of the cabinet offices.[12] The newly installed Military Government ruled by decree. One of the first of these, issued on 2 January 1917, indefinitely suspended the Dominican Congress.[13]

Creating a constabulary was one of the principle objectives of establishing Military Government and Knapp, drew up a detailed plan to accomplish this. He suggested the force be titled the *Guardia Nacional Dominicana* and urged that recruitment and training by the Marines begin at once.[14] The State Department concurred, emphasizing the importance of creating such a force, but also recommending that existing units of rural guard and frontier police be incorporated into it.[15] Some Marines, however, wanted a force that was strictly military rather than a combined military/ police constabulary. Knapp rejected this idea, arguing that the nation needed only a police force with limited military capabilities such as was being created in Haiti. Contending that it would be "many years" before Dominicans would "prefer ballots to revolutions," he said that the new *Guardia* must have a strong American commander.[16] Discussion over the exact composition and duties of the force, the selection of its American officers, and the transferring of funds from the Customs Receivership to pay for it consumed the next three months. In the interim the Marines had been busy extending their control throughout the nation and disarming local police and other armed groups.

It wasn't until April 1917 that the Military Government formally issued Executive Order 47, establishing the *Guardia* and providing $500,000 for its support.[17] Initial strength was set at 1,200 and the new force was supposed to perform police duties, guard the frontier with Haiti and aid the Marines in confronting a developing insurgency in the northeast. Its strength and training, however, were never adequate for all these tasks. As one Marine officer later noted, "it was never large enough to discharge the military functions incumbent on a national army and was too military to devote itself, except spasmodically, to its police duties."[18]

Recruiting began quickly and securing enlisted personnel proceeded rapidly. The biggest problems were the scarcity of literate recruits and poor health of many applicants. Discipline was a problem, both because most recruits had never been subject to regular discipline and because growing internal security issues cut short the time allotted for training. Clashes with civilians and breeches of discipline were frequent, leading to a high rate of courts-martial.[19]

Procuring capable officers proved even more difficult, in part because organization of the *Guardia* corresponded with the American entry into World War I. The withdrawal of some of the Marines for service in Europe combined with increasing insurgent activities led to a rapid expansion of the force. While Marine officers filled the higher posts, Marine non-commissioned officers (NCOs), few of whom spoke Spanish or had any experience leading forces of this size in combat, filled company grade posts. A few literate Dominicans were also commissioned, but they lacked training and experience. By October 1917, the Guard had 691 enlisted men, with 17 Dominican and 21 Marine officers. Most of the Marines serving as *Guardia* officers were actually NCOs.[20]

Under the circumstances, abuses were inevitable. Friction became even worse in 1918 when a new Military Governor decided to add the suppression of cockfighting to the duties of the *Guardia*. Several provincial governors quickly protested, with one declaring:

> With respect to the total suppression of cock-fighting, it is the opinion of the undersigned that this is not an opportune time, since this is the only diversion which our country people have at the present time and if they were deprived of this, they would undoubtedly turn to other more obnoxious diversions where they could be far from the vigilance of the authorities.[21]

The Military Government not only ignored such protests, but the next Governor, Rear Admiral Thomas Snowden, added suppression of prostitution to *Guardia* responsibilities.

All of this made *Guardia* tasks even more difficult and added to problems in its relations with the civilian population. *Guardia* posts in the interior took on judicial as well as police functions, with Marines serving as judges. Dominicans who were allegedly in violation of any decrees of the Military Government were tried before provost courts with few rights and a generalized presumption of guilt. They could be sentenced for anything from criticizing the Military Government to selling food above set prices.[22] There were no appeals from most of these sentences. A State Department official complained that one Marine, after a brief hearing, "which usually took place within ten minutes of the arrest," would invariably pronounce judgment by saying, "Take the son of a bitch out and bump him off."[23]

By 1919, the force's reputation was low even among the officials of the occupation. When the State Department inquired as to when the *Guardia* would be able to handle internal security by itself Minister Russell replied that it was "in no way fitted to insure law and order if our force should retire," and added that if the Marine Brigade was withdrawn "chaos will prevail."[24] In a 1919 conference between State Department and Navy Department officials, including acting Navy Secretary Franklin D. Roosevelt, there was a general consensus that the *Guardia* needed a major reorganization, with the State Department representatives stressing that, "there could be no efficiency in the *Guardia Nacional* unless it is officered by white officers and not native Dominicans."[25] Similar racial serotypes were found among the *Guardia's* Marine officers. Lieutenant Colonel Harry David, Commander of the Southern District, wrote President Harding's Executive Secretary described Dominicans as "negroes whose minds are apt to have a queer sort of turn, even in the most solemn events."[26]

Even the *Guardia's* own Commanders admitted the force's shortcomings. In an account written after he left the country, Colonel J.C. Breckinridge, who commanded the force from 1920 to 1921 noted that of the 1,300 personnel of the *Guardia* "some 300 were in jail or should be," and concluded, "An armed constabulary that is not reliable, strong and energetic is a menace instead of a security."[27] Admiral Thomas Snowden, the Military Governor, went even further, claiming that, "there can be no doubt that the loyalty of the Dominicans in the *Guardia* to the government is directly due to the presence of American troops and if left to themselves through the withdrawal of the Marines they would revert to the former insurrectionary habits."[28]

Those Dominicans who had been made officers were at times a large part of the problem. A graphic example of this is the case of 2nd Lieutenant Rafael Leonidas Trujillo. He had been commissioned on 11 January 1919 and after minimal training was put in charge of rural patrols in one of the most conflicted areas. His actions on one patrol resulted in his court-martial on charges of multiple rape and extortion. The evidence seemed overwhelming, and the only defense offered was his own denials and the remarkable claim by his Marine Defense Attorney that since the victim claimed she had been raped three times, "three times implies consent."[29] He was, nevertheless, acquitted of all charges, returned to duty, and soon thereafter promoted.[30] By the time the Marines turned over command, he was one of the forces' senior officers and later used this to propel himself into power, where he left a record as the bloodiest dictator in Caribbean history.[31]

This episode exemplified both the problem of finding qualified Dominican officers and the low standards that were expected of them. Trujillo was probably acquitted because the Marines did not want the negative publicity that his conviction would have produced and were already short of *Guardia* officers. In addition, there was virtually no precedent in Dominican history for officers being convicted for anything they did to civilians. What is even more notable is that this incident seemed to have no impact on his future career. He was simply sent to a four-month course at the newly established military academy and then steadily promoted.

Several factors contributed to a November 1920 decision to reorganize and reduce the *Guardia*. One was the rising tide of criticism by both American officials and Dominican citizens. Second was a decline in the level of internal violence, especially the insurgent activities in the east. Finally, there was a looming budget crisis. The Dominican Republic depended heavily on sugar exports for income and the price of these had

82

boomed during World War I. The Military Government took advantage of this spending heavily on roads, health, and education. The *Guardia* had shared in this largesse, and by 1919 was consuming 26.3 percent of the government's income.[32] There had been no effort to set aside money from sugar prices and once the war was over the sugar market collapsed, falling to levels much lower then before the war.[33] The financial situation also revealed some incompatibility between the goals of the occupation. Two principle objectives had been to stabilize finances and insure payments to foreign bondholders through establishing a customs receivership and organizing a professional constabulary. In keeping with the principles of the Roosevelt Corollary to the Monroe Doctrine, however, the Customs Receiver always gave first priority to paying off the bondholders, insuring that foreign government had no financial excuse for possible intervention. In times of acute financial crisis, this left little money available for the government, including the constabulary. Since the Americans would not or could not resort to such traditional remedies as not paying the enlisted men, and resisted ending the double salaries paid to Marines serving with the *Guardia,* they had to find other ways of reducing expenses. As a result, the *Guardia* was steadily reduced until, on 6 December 1921, it numbered only 77 officers and 493 enlisted men.[34] At the same time the name of the force was changed from *Guardia Nacional Dominicana* to *Policía Nacional Dominicana* (Dominican National Police).[35]

The reduction in force probably eliminated many of the force's worst offenders, though officers like Trujillo were retained. But it also substantially reduced the capacity of the force to maintain even minimal levels of internal security. One result was a proliferation of other armed bodies, some loosely attached to the *Guardia,* others generally independent. Municipal police forces, under local authorities, took over most urban policing. The large sugar producers and other wealthy rural landowners were allowed to raise their own private guards. Most significantly new units, designated as civil guards, were recruited locally, put under the command of a marine officer, and sent of to fight the insurgents. They proved more effective than either Marine or *Guardia/Policía* units, in part because of their local roots.[36]

While factors such as budget constraints undoubtedly played a role in the decisions to reorganize, reduce, and rename what became the *Policía Nacional,* there was another factor at work, the increasing disputes between the State Department and the Navy, notably Admiral Thomas Snowden, the Military Governor. He had repeatedly expressed his low opinion of Dominicans in general and their political leaders in particular. In a speech at the opening of an American-sponsored agricultural experimental station, he declared that the Military Government would last "until the generation of Dominicans then in the cradle had reached adult age."[37] He expressed similar sentiments in a message to the Secretary of the Navy, declaring that, "Dominicans have always been subjected to some form of Military Government and until they have been taught differently that is the only kind of government that can be successful." He concluded: "In my opinion, the Military Government of the United States in Santo Domingo is now and will be for at least ten years longer a necessity for the peace and prosperity of the island."[38] In another communication he refused to consider suspending the provost courts and argued that if Washington made it clear that the Military Government would last another ten or twenty years "business would receive a great impetus and encouragement."[39] At the end of 1919, under pressure from the State Department, he had appointed a Dominican advisory council, but he ignored all their recommendations, including an end to press censorship, and they all resigned at the start of 1920.[40]

Bainbridge Colby, who had replaced Robert Lansing as Secretary of State, was increasingly concerned that the occupation of the Dominican Republic, especially with growing criticism of press censorship and the actions of the provost courts, was harming US relations with the rest of Latin America and he began searching for a way to end the occupation. Russell, who had continued to be the American Minister to the Dominican Republic, but with no national government in existence had spent most of the last few years in Washington, was sent back and was instructed to begin plans for withdrawal. By November 1920, Colby had obtained President Wilson's approval for formulating a plan for gradual withdrawal.[41] In all his efforts, however, he encountered the determined opposition of Admiral Snowden. For Snowden, a weak and discredited *Guardia/Policía* served his purposes admirably, lending credence to his claims that Dominicans were incapable of maintaining order without the presence of a substantial force of Marines.

In one of the stranger anomalies of the Military Government, Admiral Snowden had dispatched a trusted aide, Lieutenant Commander Arthur H. Mayo, to Washington to act as the his representative. In many ways, this made him the equivalent of the Dominican Republic's Ambassador to the United States, a unique experience for an active duty Navy officer. He aggressively defended Snowden and denounced Dominican politicians and State Department officials. In early 1921, he wrote Snowden:

> The Navy department is now, I think, lined up flatly behind
> you. . . . This is true of Operations and at present—today—

seems so of Mr. Daniels—but he is not dependable. . . .
Then followed many interviews in Latin American Affairs
. . . Mr. Daniels had arranged an interview for me with
Mr. Davis (Norman Davis, Acting Secretary of State).
. . . When we reached Mr. Davis office and all through
the interview Mr. Daniels interrupted me—replied in the
negative on all points. . . . He brought up the two orders
issued December 6 and both he and Mr. Davis stated they
were afraid you had destroyed your further usefulness by
the issuance of them. Then I got mad—good and plenty—
and let them have it. Told them that in the first place
the orders would not have been condemned had the real
character of the people been appreciated. . . . That you had
not been taken into the confidence of the State Department
or informed in advance of their plans and that therefore
you could not be expected to know what they wanted. . . .
In the meantime I had been working on Captain Freeman
to endeavor to get better cooperation between the State
and Navy Departments—exchange of information and the
sending of orders to you through one source only—the
Navy Department. . . . Captain Freeman and I cannot talk
State Department with cussing. They are the limit and their
stand can only be understood if you take it for granted that
they are all conceited asses trying to throw a bluff to cover
the grossest, but perhaps unknowing ignorance.[42]

That a mid-ranking Navy officer would write and talk in such a manner
about his civilian superiors, including two of cabinet rank, is perhaps the
strongest evidence of just how badly relations had deteriorated not only
between the State and Navy Departments, but the Military Government
and all of Washington. Such a situation could not be permitted to endure.
Change, though, had to wait until the inauguration of President Warren G.
Harding in March 1921.

The new administration continued and expanded the policy of seeking a
way to end the occupation. The new Secretary of State, the capable Charles
Evans Hughes, and the new Navy Secretary, Edwin Denby, were able to
eliminate much of the friction between the two Departments that had
paralyzed action during the previous year. One of the first steps they took
was to replace Admiral Snowden as Military Governor with Rear Admiral
Samuel B. Robinson.[43] With Snowden went his Washington representative,
Lieutenant Commander Mayo and the atmosphere quickly improved.

Within the State Department, Sumner Welles was first charged to draw up a plan for withdrawal and was then made Special Commissioner and personal Presidential Representative to the Dominican Republic with the rank of Minister and the power to negotiate an agreement on withdrawal. As the personal representative of the President, he took precedence over all other American officials in the Republic.[44]

In June 1921, at the instructions of the State Department, the Military Government issued a Proclamation declaring that elections would be held for a new Dominican government and expressing the "hope that the withdrawal may be completed . . . within a period of eight months."[45] Issued on 14 June, this declaration received what the American Minister described as "a hot blast of protest from the press, advising the people not to accept it as this would imply sanction of past wrongs."[46] Most Dominican political leaders echoed the reaction of the press and the scheduled elections had to be postponed. It would be thirty-nine, not eight months, before the Marines finally left.

With Snowden and Mayo finally out of the way and the State Department again in firm control over Dominican policy two major obstacles remained before the Marines could be withdrawn. The first was reaching some sort of agreement with the increasingly anti-American political leaders of the Republic. The second was getting the long neglected *Policía Nacional* in a position to provide basic security. Work on this task began almost immediately.

In order to better prepare Dominicans to take command of the *Policía*, the Marines established the Haina Military Academy and its first class was admitted in August. Many of the initial students were already serving as officers, but the four-month Academy class gave them at least a brief exposure to the duties of a professional officer. In the next three years it turned out a steady stream of graduates, providing the necessary material to fill all the *Policía's* officer slots. While new officers were being trained part of the task of dealing with the still smoldering insurgency was turned over to small patrols of the civic guards. Their activity, combined with an amnesty program, finally began to restore peace to this region in the spring of 1922.[47] This made the task that the *Policía* would face considerably easier. They could now concentrate on routine rural patrolling, guarding the frontier with Haiti, and enforcing the law outside of the larger towns. This also provided an opportunity for them to begin repairing their badly damaged image.

While relations with Robison were not nearly as conflictive as they had been with Snowden, there were still major points of disagreement. Welles found himself constantly trying to balance the position of the Military Government with the demands of the Dominicans. He brought considerable diplomatic skills and a great deal of personal patience and determination to this task. In the final analysis, though, when disputes seemed irreconcilable, he more often than not sided with the demands of the Dominicans.[48] Admiral Robison was not concerned with extending the occupation, as his predecessor had been, and evidenced no interest in continuing the crusades against cockfighting and prostitution. His concerns were largely those of a military professional, notably insuring the safety of his own forces and maintaining security in his area of responsibility. Political problems rarely entered into his calculations.[49]

One additional complicating factor emerged with the 1921 visit to the Republic of the Senate Committee charged with investigating the occupations of the Dominican Republic and Haiti. Senator Medill McCormick, the Committee Chair, was frustrated in his efforts to help negotiate an accord on a plan of evacuation and informed the State Department that the occupation might need to continue for up to three more years and that a primary task during that period must be the training of Dominican officers for the *Policía Nacional*.[50]

Negotiations between Welles and Dominican leaders was complicated by their extreme distrust of the Military Government, by the Dominicans' own bitter factional divisions, and by Washington's insistence that any evacuation agreement include Dominican acceptance of the actions and decrees of the Military Government. Leadership and training of the *Policía* was also a continuing issue and led to frequent disputes not only between Welles and the Dominicans but between the State and Navy Departments. On 25 January 1922, Welles informed Hughes that the situation was "growing constantly more unsatisfactory," and suggested that Robison inform the Dominican leaders that if an agreement wasn't reached on installing a provisional government the Military Government would continue "until such time as the urgent public works have been completed and an adequate Dominican constabulary is functioning." He also recommended that Washington stop insisting on the retention of an American military mission that would remain in charge of training the constabulary after the occupation ended. At the end of this message, Admiral Robison added that he concurred.[51]

Negotiations remained largely stalemated through the spring of 1922. On 16 March, Robison, acting on instructions from Hughes, issued a proclamation that the Military Government would continue until at least July 1924.[52] This may have convinced some Dominican leaders that they had to adopt a more flexible approach in negotiations. Welles resigned from the State Department, but was quickly sent back to the Dominican Republic as American Commissioner with full powers. Negotiations proceeded steadily over the installation of a provisional government that would then conduct national elections, but this raised new concerns on the part of Admiral Robison. In a letter to Welles, he advanced a plan to maintain the US military presence under the provisional government to insure order and continue training the *Policía*. US forces would only intervene on the request of the provisional government or if "the situation fell apart completely." He saw the alternatives as either adopting his plan or pulling out completely. He also inquired as to whether the United States saw the Dominicans as friends or enemies, arguing that if they were enemies we must guard against any surprise actions on their part.[53]

As negotiations with the Dominicans progressed, friction between Welles and Robison, notably over security issues, increased. The Dominicans insisted that when a provisional government was installed all Marine officers should be withdrawn from the *Policía*. Robison reluctantly agreed, but insisted that training be left in Marine hands and that the Military Government alone approve all candidates for officer's commissions.[54] The Dominicans ultimately agreed to Marine control over officer training, something Robison attributed to their discovering that, "they did not have enough officers of their own," adding, "The Dominicans are suspicious of us and do not want us."[55]

Robison protested Welles' plan to withdraw the Marines from most of the Republic, concentrating their forces in the three principal cities and confining them all to their barracks on election day, but his protests were all overruled. So, too, were his efforts to continue press censorship and to block the release of political prisoners, to obtain a one-year extension of American instruction of the *Policía*, and to have the Military Government continue to exercise some control over the government's budget. Finally, the Navy Department had to tell him not to make any further suggestions.[56] He was recalled to Washington two days before the provisional government took office and was replaced by the senior Marine officer in the Republic, Brigadier General Harry Lee.

One area where Robison and Welles were in agreement was on the need for continued Marine training, and here they were largely able to overcome Dominican objections. The agreement establishing the provisional government left training of both officers and enlisted recruits in the hands of the Military Government. As for the force itself, the provisional government would appoint its higher officers, but there was the expectation, or at least the hope, that these would be steadily replaced by Marine-trained officers.[57] Two last minute decrees from the Military government further defined the status of the *Policía.* The first declared that the *Policía Nacional Dominicana* would be the nation's only armed force and gave control over assignments and promotions to the civilian Secretary of State for the Interior and Police. The second, issued just twelve days before the provisional government's inauguration, reversed this giving that power to the colonel-commander of the *Policía.* Probably designed as a hedge against political manipulation of the force this actually set the stage for the rise to national power of its commander.[58]

The first Dominican commander of the *Policía* was General Buenaventura Cabral, a provincial governor with no ties to the major political parties. He and the other nominees for senior posts were given a few weeks of Marine indoctrination before assuming their duties when the new government was inaugurated on 21 October 1922.[59] General Lee retained the title of Military Governor, but his limited powers were largely confined to security issues.

It would be July 1924 before a constitutional Dominican government was elected and installed and two months after that before the last of the Marines departed. This period went relatively smoothly. There were none of the major conflicts within the American policy community that had characterized earlier periods. General Lee emphasized the need to minimize friction between the Marines and the national population and effectively disciplined those who disobeyed his instructions.[60] The provost courts had been eliminated when the Marines were concentrated in the major cities and this removed a major source of Dominican complaints. Welles reported in April 1923:

> I feel that the relations between the provisional government and the military government are exceedingly satisfactory. The President advises me that the attitude of the military government under General Lee has been consistently helpful and has been little or no disagreement. . . . The increase of efficiency of the national police has exceeded the most optimistic expectations of the military government and the relations between the American officers in command of the training centers and the Dominican officers in command of the field forces are entirely harmonious.[61]

There, were of course, some problems. General Lee, supported by Welles, was concerned that the Navy, evidently assuming that its mission was essentially completed, had begun withdrawing officers assigned to training the *Policía* and was not replacing them. Welles argued that the training was an obligation undertaken by the United States and that, "no greater service could be given the Dominican people." He urged the State Department to take the matter up with the Navy.[62] Evidently this had the desired effect as there seem to have been no further complaints.

Following the election there was an effort to retain some Marines to continue training the force. At first, this seemed to be going well, but ultimately the President-elect, Horacio Vásquez, introduced so many conditions and restrictions that the Marines decided they could not undertake the task and the officers assigned to training withdrew with the rest of the Marines in September 1924.[63]

The fate of the *Policía* after the Marines withdrew would be a disappointment to its American creators and a disaster for hopes for Dominican democracy. Central to this was the career of Rafael L. Trujillo. When the Marines left, he was the third-ranking Dominican officer of the *Policía* and before the year was out he was his chief of staff. By June 1925, he had been promoted to colonel and was the force's commandant. Two years later, he was made a Brigadier General and the *Policía Nacional* were renamed the National Army.[64] By adroit maneuvering he managed to first force the ouster of the president, then had himself "elected" president in 1930. Once in office, he rapidly expanded the army, ending its police functions by creating a new national police. This force, in turn, replaced all existing local police forces, centralizing power in his hands. A huge intelligence service was created, opposition was ruthlessly repressed, and, in 1937, an estimated 15,000 Haitian peasants, residing in the Republic, were massacred. Army equipment was updated and compulsory military service instituted.[65]

Trujillo hung onto power by a combination of ruthless terror, extravagant spending on the military which was allowed to engage in a wide variety of corrupt practices, and by doing whatever was necessary to stay in Washington's good graces.[66] This worked until the late 1950s. By then his tyranny had become so obvious and US concerns about the rise to power of Castro in Cuba so central that he had become both an embarrassment and an obstacle in Washington's eyes. In May 1961, he was assassinated by a group of Dominicans with the support of the CIA.[67] His family tried to hang on to power as had the Somozas in Nicaragua, but a combination of political pressures and the threat of military intervention by the Kennedy administration forced them out and led to the inauguration of Juan Bosch as Dominican president. Seven months later the military overthrew him and took over the government.[68] In April 1965, an uprising by a dissident military faction supporting the return of Bosch threatened to turn into a civil war. Fearful that Castro might take advantage of the situation, the United States intervened, first on its own, then with the cooperation of a few Latin American nations, notably Brazil. Months of uncertainty, negotiations and sporadic violence followed before the leaders of both military factions were sent into exile, and new elections held.[69]

The elections brought to power Joaquín Balaguer, an aging but crafty politician. Although there were rumors of coups, he managed, by mixture of dividing authority and overlooking corruption, to keep the military largely out of politics for the next two decades. His successors, benefitting from the hemisphere-wide move to civilian rule, have kept the military under tighter control.[70]

Divided American authority and the vague and shifting purposes of the occupation constantly hampered the US creation of a constabulary force in the Dominican Republic. The Military Government produced stability, but at a very high price. The force it created was the most powerful and unified in Dominican history and was able to bring to an end the power of regional *caudillos* and the era of political civil wars. But in the process it became a potential political power itself and in the hands of a ruthless individual became the instrument of establishing one of the worst and longest lasting dictatorships in Latin America. The remarkably smooth transition to national command was a significant accomplishment, but the failure to leave behind any mechanism for establishing effective civil control over the force undid any good this may have produced. Dr. Bruce Calder, author of the best study of the Occupation, concluded, "foreign intervention, as practiced by the United States in the Dominican Republic from 1916 to 1924, was a policy neither wise nor just, a policy unproductive for all concerned."[71]

Notes

1. For details, see William Javier Nelson, *Almost a Territory: America's Attempt to Annex the Dominican Republic* (Newark, DE: University of Delaware Press, 1990).

2. Theodore Roosevelt to Joseph Bucklin Bishop, 23 February 1904, quoted in Dana Gardner Munro, *Intervention and Dollar Diplomacy in the Caribbean, 1900–1921* (Princeton, NJ: Princeton University Press, 1964), 91.

3. Theodore Roosevelt, "State of the Union Address," 5 December 1905, http://www.theodoreroosevelt.com.

4. Munro, *Intervention*, 116–121.

5. Sumner Welles, *Naboth's Vineyard: The Dominican Republic, 1844–1924*, Vol. II (New York, NY: Payson and Clarke Ltd., 1928), 722 and 734–743.

6. William Russell to Dominican Foreign Office, 19 November 1915, *Papers Relating to Foreign Relations of the United States* (Washington, DC: Government Printing Office, 1916), 333–337.

7. Russell to Secretary of State Lansing, 6 May and 7 May 1916, *Papers Relating to Foreign Relations of the United States* (Washington, DC: Government Printing Office, 1916), 224–225; Munro, *Intervention*, 306.

8. Admiral William B. Caperton, "Activities of Rear Admiral William B. Caperton, US Navy, while in command of Cruiser Squadron, US Atlantic Fleet and Commander in Chief, US Pacific Fleet," Papers of William B. Caperton, Naval Historical Foundation Collection, Manuscript Division, Library of Congress, 256.

9. Bruce J. Calder, *The Impact of Intervention: The Dominican Republic during the U.S. Occupation of 1916–1924* (Austin, TX: University of Texas Press, 1984), 10–12.

10. Memorandum of Conference between Admiral Benson, Captain Knapp, Mr. Polk, Minister Russell, and Mr. Stabler, 31 October 1916, National Archives and Record Service, Naval Records Collection of the Office of Naval Records and Library, RG 45, Subject File WH 7.

11. Proclamation of Occupation and Military Government," 29 November 1916, *Papers Relating to Foreign Relations of the United States* (Washington, DC: Government Printing Office, 1916), 246–247.

12. Knapp to Secretary of the Navy, 8 December 1916, RG 59, 839.00/1972; Daniels to Knapp, 8 December 1916, RG 59, 839.00/1972; Knapp to Daniels, 8 December 1916, National Archives and Record Service, Records of the United States Department of State, RG 59, 839.00/1972.

13. Marvin Goldwert, *The Constabulary in the Dominican Republic and Nicaragua: Progeny and Legacy of United States Intervention* (Gainesville, FL: University of Florida Press, 1962), 7.

14. Knapp to Secretary of the Navy, 12 December 1916, RG 59, 839.1051/8 (enclosure).

15. Memorandum by Stabler for Secretary of State, 10 January 1917, RG 59, 839.1051/8.

16. Knapp to Secretary of Navy, 14 January 1917, RG 59, 839.00/1985.

17. Goldwert, 8.
18. Colonel Rufus Lane, quoted in Calder, 55.
19. Calder, 56.
20. Goldwert, 12.
21. Nasario Suardi, Governor of La Vega, to the Officer in Charge, Department of Interior and Police, 3 June 1918. This material was originally in the Marine Corps Archives at the Washington Navy Yard, but has since been transferred to the National Archives, RG 38, Records of the Military Government of Santo Domingo.
22. For a detailed discussion of the provost courts and of Dominican reactions to them see Marvin A. Soloman, "Law, Order and Justice in the Dominican Republic During the United States Military Government, 1916 to 1924" (M.A. thesis, Department of Historical Studies, Southern Illinois University–Edwardsville, 1969).
23. Herbert Gould to Acting Secretary of State Phillips, 18 August 1918, RG 59, 839.1051/16.
24. Russell to Lansing, 8 August 1919, *Papers Relating to Foreign Relations of the United States*, Vol. II (Washington, DC: Government Printing Office, 1919), 120.
25. Memorandum by J.C. Dunn, State Department Division of Latin American Affairs, Conference held on 8 April 1919, RG 59, 839.1051/17.
26. Lieutenant Colonel Harry David to George Christian, Executive Secretary to President Harding, 10 July 1921, Papers of Warren G. Harding, Ohio State Historical Archives, Columbus, Ohio.
27. Colonel J.C. Breckinridge, "The Guardia Nacional Dominicana, 1920–21," Papers of J.C. Breckinridge, Marine Corps Historical Archives, Quantico, VA.
28. Snowden to the Secretary of the Navy, 23 June 1919, RG 59, 839.1051/20.
29. The complete trial transcript can be found in General Records of the Navy Department, RG 80, File 16870–47:477.
30. For a discussion of the trial and its aftermath, see Richard L. Millett and Marvin Soloman, "The Court Martial of Lieutenant Rafael L. Trujillo," *Revista/ Review Interamericana*, Vol. II, No. 3 (Fall 1972), 396–404.
31. The best study of Trujillo's career is Robert D. Crassweller, *Trujillo: The Life and Times of a Caribbean Dictator*, (New York, NY: MacMillan Company, 1966).
32. Goldwert, 12.
33. For a highly critical discussion of the economic crisis and its impact on the *Guardia*, see Breckinridge, 11–14.
34. Goldwert, 13.
35. Ibid., 19.
36. Calder, 176–177.
37. Quoted in Welles, 820.
38. Snowden to the Secretary of the Navy, 23 June 1919, RG 59, 839.1051/20.
39. Snowden to Russell, 12 February 1919, *Papers Relating to Foreign*

Relations of the United States (Washington, DC: Government Printing Office, 1919), 141–144.

40. Munro, *Intervention*, 321.

41. Munro, *The United States and the Caribbean Republics*, 45.

42. Commander Arthur H. Mayo to Snowden, 27 January 1921, National Archives, Records of the Military Government of Santo Domingo, Miscellaneous Correspondence, RG 38.

43. David Charles MacMichael, "The United States and the Dominican Republic, 1871–1940: A Cycle in Caribbean Diplomacy" (Ph.D. dissertation, University of Oregon, 1964), 543.

44. Kenneth J. Grieb, "Warren G. Harding and the Dominican Republic: U.S. Withdrawal, 1921–1923," *Journal of Inter-American Studies*, Vol. XI, No. 3 (July 1969), 433.

45. "Draft of Proclamation for Withdrawal of American Forces from the Dominican Republic," *Papers Relating to Foreign Relations of the United States*, Vol. I (Washington, DC: Government Printing Office, 1921), 837.

46. Russell to the Secretary of State, 14 June 1921, *Papers Relating to Foreign Relations of the United States*, Vol. I (Washington, DC: Government Printing Office, 1921), 838.

47. Calder, 176–178.

48. Welles included a lengthy description of his efforts to negotiate a withdrawal in his massive, two-volume history of the Dominican Republic, *Naboth's Vineyard* (New York, NY: Payson and Clarke, 1928).

49. Grieb, 434.

50. Senator Medill McCormick to Hughes, 16 December 1821, RG 59, 639.00/2456.

51. Welles to Hughes, 25 January 1922, RG 59, 839.00/2465.

52. Welles, *Naboth's Vineyard*, 852–853.

53. Robison to Welles, 11 August 1922, RG 59, 839.1051/25.

54. Secretary of the Navy Denby to Hughes, 14 September 1922, RG 59, 839.1051/26.

55. Robison to Captain F.H. Clark, USN, Office of Naval Operations, 20 September 1922, RG 45, Subject File WH–7.

56. MacMichael, 573–574.

57. Munro, *The United States and the Caribbean Republics*, 57–58.

58. Goldwert, 20.

59. Munro, *The United States and the Caribbean Republics*, 58–59.

60. Calder, 234.

61. Welles to Hughes, 5 April 1923, RG 59, 839.00/2692

62. Welles to Hughes, 30 April 1923, RG 59, 839.1051/29.

63. Munro, *The United States and the Caribbean Republics*, 65.

64. Crassweller, 48–51.

65. Howard Wiarda, *Dictatorship and Development: The Methods of Control in Trujillo's Dominican Republic* (Gainesville, FL: University of Florida Press, 1968), 43–45.

66. For an extensive, well-researched discussion of Trujillo's relations with the American military, see Bernardo Vega, *Trujillo y las Fuerzas Armadas Norteamericanos* (Santo Domingo, Dominican Republic: Fundación Cultural Dominicana, 1992).

67. Tim Weiner, *Legacy of Ashes: The History of the CIA* (New York, NY: Doubleday, 2007), 171–172.

68. For a discussion of this chaotic period, see John Bartlow Martin, *Overtaken by Events* (Garden City, NY: Doubleday, 1966).

69. For a discussion of these events, see Martin, 637–703. For an excellent study of the US intervention, see Lawrence A. Yates, *Power Pack: U.S. Intervention in the Dominican Republic, 1965–1966* (Fort Leavenworth, KS: Combat Studies Institute Press, 1988).

70. For a discussion of the military since 1966, see Jonathan Hartlyn, *The Struggle for Democratic Politics in the Dominican Republic* (Chapel Hill, NC: University of North Carolina Press, 1998), 123–126, 146–149, 159, and 313

71. Calder, 252.

Chapter 7

Nicaragua: Limited Success and Costly Failures

No nation in Central America has provided as many foreign policy dilemmas or caused as much frustration as Nicaragua. From the filibustering expeditions of William Walker in the 1850s until the present day efforts to deal with the governments of President Daniel Ortega, Washington has repeatedly tried to direct and reshape Nicaraguan politics with little if any success. At the heart of many of these efforts have been dealings with Nicaragua's security forces.

Nicaragua, prior to the 1990s, never had a true national army or nonpolitical police. Up until 1926, most forces were simply armed instruments of partisan politics, with little training or discipline and a reputation for being largely instruments of individual political ambitions. From 1926 until the end of 1932, police and military were combined into a national guard under foreign command, serving to support an American intervention. From 1933 until 1936, the force experienced numerous internal conflicts, resulting in its domination by another ambitious individual, Anastasio Somoza García. He used it to seize political power that he and his sons held until 1979. That year, the guard was totally destroyed by a Marxist insurgency, the Frente Sandinista de Liberación Nacional (FSLN). The insurgents became the army and police, and this highly partisan force soon found itself in a civil conflict against US-backed counter-revolutionaries. Only when the FSLN lost power in the 1990 presidential elections did the military and police begin to assume a national, nonpolitical orientation and even then the transition was slow and difficult.

Direct United States military involvement began with the 1912 intervention by units of Marines and armed sailors. This ended a civil conflict and essentially destroyed the rebel forces, but provided no guarantee of future stability. Determined to prevent civil conflicts, the United States left a company-sized force in Managua, ostensibly to guard the American legation, but actually to serve as an indicator of Washington's refusal to tolerate efforts at armed revolution.[1]

The minority Conservative Party, which had been installed in power by the US intervention, used the Marine presence to rig elections and oppress the opposition Liberals. From 1913 until 1925, Nicaragua was also able to have one of smallest military forces and budgets in Latin America. By 1924, the army had only 37 officers and 329 enlisted men. There were also 934 national police, a force whose main occupation seemed to be harassing opposition political figures.[2] The 1925 military budget was only $132,571 with another $194,704 designated for the police, less than a quarter of what its notably peaceful neighbor, Costa Rica, was spending.[3]

In 1923, the State Department brought representatives of the five Central American nations (Panama was not considered part of Central America) to Washington for a conference on Arms Limitation. The five nations agreed to limit the size of their armies and, under considerable US pressure, to "establish a National Guard to cooperate with existing Armies in the preservation of order." They also promised to "give consideration to the employment of suitable instructors in order to take advantage, in this manner, of experience acquired in other countries in organizing such corps."[4] Washington clearly saw this as referring to Americans given their experience in the Philippines and in other Latin American nations.

Creation of such constabulary forces was an American project and most of the Central Americans ignored this provision after they left Washington. El Salvador did create a National Guard to maintain order in rural areas, but hired Spanish rather than American instructors to train it. This force in no way replaced the regular army. In fact its officers were graduates of the same military academy as regular army officers and it was under the military high command.[5] Over time, it became known for corruption and extreme brutality in defending the interests of the rural oligarchy.

Only in Nicaragua was the United States able to move its project of creating a constabulary forward. In 1924, that nation was experiencing something of a political crisis. Splits within both traditional parties had led to the formation of an uneasy coalition between factions of both traditional parties. The new president, Carlos Solórzano, faced bitter opposition from the Conservatives powerful military caudillo, General Emiliano Chamorro. So as soon as he took office he asked the State Department to suspend its plans to withdraw the legation guard. The Department agreed with the proviso that the new administration move quickly to create an American-trained constabulary. Solórzano wasn't enthusiastic about American proposals, but fear of Chamorro, who strongly opposed the idea and US pressures, led him reluctantly to support a law creating the new force. As passed by Nicaragua's Congress the final bill watered down US proposals, limiting the authority of foreign trainers, and giving control over the supply system, traditionally a major source of graft, to the Minister of Police. The new "*Guardia Nacional*" was defined as "an urban, rural and judicial police force," with no mention made of its replacing the existing army.[6]

While far from what was hoped for, Washington decided to accept this plan and proceeded to select a retired US Army Major, Calvin B. Carter, who had helped train the Philippine Constabulary, to command the Guard. To assist him an additional four American's were selected as his assistants. Unlike previous Nicaraguan security forces, his force was to be recruited voluntarily, have regular pay, uniforms, and training, and was supposed to be open to all qualified citizens, not just supporters of the party in power.

Carter arrived in Nicaragua on 16 July 1925, less than three weeks before the last Marines departed. Of the original 200 recruits, nearly half failed their entrance physicals. The force lacked weapons and supplies, but the nervous president wanted them rushed into service, patrolling the streets of the capitol and serving as his personal guard.[7]

Just over a month after Carter arrived, Nicaragua was plunged into political turmoil. Supporters of General Chamorro seized his War Minister, General José María Moncada, and other Liberals in the government, then demanded that the President purge all Liberals from his cabinet. Despite promises of support from Major Carter, Solórzano gave in. A few days later, Chamorro seized control of the principal army post in Managua then demanded that all remaining Liberals be removed from the government and that he be made commanding general of the army. Again, Solórzano caved in.

Chamorro, who had previously opposed the constabulary, now became its strong supporter, urging its expansion. The US Minister to Nicaragua, Charles Eberhardt, explained this change of heart:

> Logically enough, the ins are usually in favor of a well-trained Constabulary. . . . It is doubtful if in these countries such an organization, free from politics, is ever wanted, but rather one made up largely of men of the same political faith as is held by those in power. Thus General Chamorro and the Conservatives as a whole, who formerly opposed strengthening the organization, now recommend its increase by several hundred men and their continued training under Major Carter.[8]

Chamorro now moved steadily to place himself in total power. He had the congress purged of its Liberal members and the vice president, Liberal Juan Bautista Sacasa, fled into exile, fearing for his life. The rump congress promptly declared that office vacant and selected Chamorro as first designate to succeed the president. On 16 January, that same body granted the president an indefinite leave of absence and just over two months later he formally resigned. The United States, committed to a policy of not recognizing Central American regimes that took power by non-constitutional means, brushed aside the legal façade Chamorro had erected and announced it would not recognize his government now or in the future.[9] Encouraged by this and by the absence of the Marines the Liberals promptly began preparations for an uprising.

Chamorro now frantically tried to build up the guard, abandoning any pretense of nonpartisanship in the process. The American Minister reported that that force was "fast disintegrating into a politically controlled machine for the present regime."[10] He later noted:

> It is very apparent that the time has not yet come, if it ever will, when a nonpartisan constabulary or National Guard, organized and maintained under American ideas and ideals, will be a success in Nicaragua. It is not wanted. Just as the President may be Conservative or Liberal, so will he insist that the organization be made up of men of his following.[11]

While Chamorro managed to contain the initial Liberal uprisings others followed and his government began to lose control. The State Department, suspicious of Mexican support for the Liberals, but determined not to recognize Chamorro, found itself with a major policy dilemma. An effort to negotiate a settlement, held on the USS *Denver*, broke down on Liberal instance that Sacasa become President. Meanwhile, the Guard fought reasonably well, but was steadily decimated. Major Carter left Nicaragua and the regime appeared about to collapse.

Chamorro finally resigned and his temporary replacement agreed to restore the twenty-one ousted Liberals to the Congress. Only three, however, returned. The congress, with US support, then selected former President Adolfo Díaz, who had been in office during the 1912 intervention, as President and Washington recognized him three days later. This did nothing to deter the Liberal forces that continued to gain ground.

American forces had begun to land in Nicaragua in mid-January, and, by 15 March 1927, there were nearly 2,000 Marines and sailors in Nicaragua, ostensibly to protect foreign lives and property. But the Liberals continued to advance and the United States seemed to have to choose between an all-out occupation and allowing Díaz to be overthrown. Trying to find a third option, President Coolidge sent former Secretary of War Henry L. Stimson to Nicaragua, backed by the threat of US force, to negotiate an end to the conflict.

Initial negotiations with Liberal political leaders foundered on US insistence that Díaz remain in office through the 1928 elections. Stimson then went directly to General Moncada, their principal military commander. Faced with the threat of all-out intervention, Moncada ultimately agreed to a package of agreements, including restoration of local Liberal political officials, a disarmament of both his and the government's forces, US supervision of the 1928 elections, and the replacement of existing army and police by a new National Guard, officered and trained by Americans.[12] All but one of Moncada's Generals accepted this plan. The refusal of a relatively minor commander, Augusto César Sandino, to disarm did not, at the time, arouse much concern.

Without waiting for a formal agreement with the Nicaraguan government, the Marines quickly set about recruiting and organizing the new *Guardia Nacional*. The remnants of the old Guard were dissolved, but many immediately enlisted in the new force. Recruiting formally began on 24 May 1927 and within a month three companies had been organized and a Marine Colonel had assumed the rank of Nicaraguan Brigadier General and the title *Jefe Director de la Guardia Nacional de Nicaragua*.[13] The original plan was to give recruits several months of training, then slowly have them replace Marines throughout the country, but this quickly foundered when Sandino began to attack the government.

Sandino's forces were concentrated in the rural province of Nueva Segovia, near the Honduran border. Stimson had suggested that an Army cavalry regiment be sent to the region, but the Navy and Marines opposed this, with Brigadier General Logan Feland, the Marine commander in Nicaragua noting that they "didn't want any of the Army down here."[14] Sandino still was not taken seriously until, in late June, he seized an American-owned gold mine and took several hundred pounds of dynamite. Hurriedly, the newly organized First Company of the *Guardia* was dispatched to Ocotal. Shortly after they arrived, Sandino launched an all-out attack on the town that lasted for nearly two days and was only beaten off with the support of Marine aircraft dispatched from Managua.[15]

Fighting Sandino would occupy the majority of the *Guardia* for the next five and half years, but it did not release them from their other mission of taking over policing duties. The Marines put in charge of this were ill-prepared for such a mission and encountered a host of difficulties. A colorful account of some of these was later recorded by the first to serve as Managua's Chief of Police:

> The first few days were spent getting in touch with the
> old police force. . . . Well it was run mostly by graft. . . .
> We had to study up on existing police laws and how to cut
> thru red tape to get convictions. I had four junior officers

assigned who could read, write and speak Spanish. . . . To get the office going we had to borrow, bum and swipe what we needed.

I immediately started schools and had the lieutenants go over with the men the police laws then in force. The policeman was taught first to know what is wrong and then to know what to do about it. Their idea of the job was to lock up everybody they had a grudge against or who would not turn over to them a little graft. Well we had to weed out the undesirables at the start before we got a write up in the paper. . . . We worked on the newspaper men and got something on them and they left us alone.

In the beginning the police force was armed with the rifle and the bayonet. We immediately discarded that because we had several policemen cut by their own bayonets. . . . We then had several cases where the policeman was justified in shooting his rifle, but the bullet, after hitting the fugitive, would continue on and hit an innocent bystander. . . . We turned to and armed them with clubs and pistols.

The people were against us at first because they could not bribe us to look blind or the other way. I used the lady next to the police station (Mrs. Irene de Pasos) to present our case to the President (Díaz) whenever we had to lock up some prominent Conservative or once in a while his nephew or brother or his secretary. . . .

I hope it is possible . . . to have the Marine Corps get up a pamphlet on practical police work. . . . I believe it should be made part of the law course in the Marine Corps Schools in Quantico. It is very important when the Marines capture a place for the Navy in a foreign country that we have officers competent to handle one of the most important functions in getting in touch with the natives. Also in taking over a foreign city allowance should be made for differences in race, customs, laws, language and habits of the natives, until they get used to us.[16]

Slow progress in training, budget issues, and the growing preoccupation with fighting Sandino meant that the Guardia was slow in taking over police functions, especially in outlying provinces. In the Department of Chontales, for example, the local police remained in place until mid-1928.

When the Guard took over the number of arrests, the amount of fines, and weapons seized increased more than twenty-fold, something which some segments of the population appreciated and others did not.[17]

While the initial recruiting and training was going on and the combat with Sandino had begun the negotiation and ratification of a formal agreement establishing the Guard continued to languish. Marine Generals John Lejeune and Logan Feland had prepared a draft treaty that the State Department approved. But the Díaz administration tried to make several basic changes, including filling the ranks through compulsory rather than voluntary service, and creating separate military and police forces. The Conservatives were especially strong in wanting to retain locally controlled police, hoping to use these to influence the 1928 elections. The State Department rejected all these proposals. The Liberals generally supported the treaty, believing it would enhance their chances of success in the 1928 elections, and even wanted the United States to agree to train the Guardia for twelve years. All of this was rejected and the agreement was finally signed on 22 December 1927.[18] Final ratification was repeatedly delayed in the Nicaraguan Congress, but the United States simply operated as if the treaty was in full force.

The treaty provide for a force of 93 officers, initially all Americans, and 1,136 enlisted men with an annual budget of $689,132. Provisions were included for expanding both with these numbers declared to be "the minimum requirements for the Guardia Nacional de Nicaragua." Other provisions declared that the force would be "the sole military and police force of the Republic." Its commander, with the title of Jefe Director, was given control over "recruiting, appointment, instruction, training, promotions, examination, discipline, operation of troops, clothing, rations, arms and equipment, quarters and administration." American officers serving in the Guardia were exempted from the jurisdiction of Nicaraguan courts and those Americans serving with the force would all be appointed by the US President.[19]

Organizing and training this new force presented a wide variety of problems. Recruits were supposed to be able to pass a physical examination and be literate, but STDs, parasites, and other afflictions were widespread and large numbers failed the physicals. Once in the Guardia these problems persisted, with the Medical Department reporting 487 new reported cases of venereal disease among enlisted men in 1932 alone, a figure representing nearly a quarter of the total enlisted strength. Only malaria, with 804 cases, represented a more serious problem. Literate recruits were extremely scarce and that requirement was largely overlooked, with the Guard instead setting up schools to teach enlisted men basic literacy.[20]

Finding officers presented a different set of problems. As an incentive to Marines, those assigned to the Guardia drew both their Marine pay and Nicaraguan government pay. Since they normally served one or two ranks higher in the Guardia than in the Corps, this represented a major increase. But, with the Corps occupied in Haiti and China, and depression restrictions on funding, there were never enough available officers. As had been the practice elsewhere, this meant that most of the junior officer slots were filled by Marine NCOs. While dedicated and courageous, most of these had limited education and often little command of Spanish. They usually proved effective in combat, but were less capable in many areas of training, especially those related to inculcating national loyalties and nonpartisan sentiments in the troops.

Medical duties were to be handled by Navy doctors and Corpsmen, but these were also in limited supply and Nicaraguan contract physicians eventually did much of the work. This may have had an unforeseen advantage as this part of the Guardia had fewer problems when the time came to change over to Nicaraguan command.

Following the battle at Ocotal, Sandino was relatively inactive for a time, but his activities increased steadily beginning in late 1927. The Guardia reported three clashes in November and eight in December. In January 1928, there were ten and in February eight. There were even more with Marine units. There was some decline in late 1928 and 1929, and the Marines were largely withdrawn from combat. But violence escalated dramatically beginning in 1930 with 132 clashes, between Guardia units and Sandino's forces, followed by 141 clashes in 1931 and 176 in 1932.[21]

The Guardia generally performed well in these combats and the casualties inflicted on Sandino's forces were much greater than those they suffered. But the strains of combat, disrupted training, reduced attention to policing functions, and contributed to problems between the Guardia, civilian populations, and the general public. It also led to a bitter hatred of Sandino by most of the Guardia. The United States and the Guardia helped run relatively free and honest elections in Nicaragua in 1928. The head of the electoral Commission sent by Washington to oversee the elections was an Army Brigadier General, Frank McCoy, and most of his assistants were also Army officers.[22] President Díaz, at the request of the State Department, gave control over the Guardia to McCoy, an action that upset the senior Navy and Marine officers in the area. McCoy also began investigating the overall military situation. Admiral David Foote Sellers, the senior US

104

Naval official in the area, grew increasingly upset with McCoy's tendency to criticize the Marines and to issue orders directly to the Guardia, bypassing the regular chain of command. As friction increased, some began to fear that McCoy would try to replace the Marines with Army personnel. Colonel L. McCarty Little, Director of Marine Corps Operations and Training, wrote a memorandum arguing that:

> To take from the Navy a problem it has successfully handled for century and to assign such duty to the Army, of whose functions it is not properly a part would be uneconomic to say the least. An Army officer assigned in charge of the problems of Nicaragua would under the present depend entirely . . . upon the support of a service with whose technical limitations he is not wholly familiar. Why introduce this possibly jarring note? . . . To assign Army officers to the Guardia Nacional is to introduce an additional system of training. . . . Army officers detailed for duty under Marines would require instruction in our special type of training. Army training placed over a Marine system would to a large degree undo the results of last year's work.[23]

Sellers supported Little's stand noting that:

> I am very decidedly of the opinion that the best results will not be obtained by mixing the Army with the Navy and Marine Corps in matters like the present operation. . . . To import a lot of Army officers whose standards, traditions and methods differ from ours does not tend to promote harmony, efficiency or develop esprit de corps.[24]

While these inter-service rivalries proved largely ephemeral problems with the victor in the 1928 elections, President José María Moncada, were much more concrete. Unlike the compliant Díaz, who owed his position to the Americans, Moncada felt no such debt. He was determined both to assert his independence and to expand his powers. Shortly after his inauguration he began calling for the formation of a "Volunteer Army" under officers appointed by him to support the fight against Sandino. The American Minister and the Marine Jefe Director of the Guardia objected, but Moncada, supported by the Marine's commander, General Feland, began recruiting his volunteers. Two columns, accompanied by Marines, were ultimately dispatched to Northern Nicaragua where they accomplished little in a military sense, but did arouse alarm among many Marines because of their habit of shooting prisoners. Word of these actions reached the State Department, where Henry Stimson had just become Secretary, and he quickly began urging Moncada to disband the volunteer troops. In June, the Nicaraguan President reluctantly complied with this request, but did not abandon his schemes to create a force under his control.[25]

The 1927 Guardia Agreement was finally ratified by the Nicaraguan Congress on 19 February 1929, but Moncada was able to get several amendments added, including some which seemed to give local officials the power to issue orders to the Guard, others which could limit the force to the size specified in the original agreement and one which required all Marines serving as Guard officers to have a working knowledge of Spanish.[26] The State Department rejected all these amendments, convinced that their true intent was to undermine the Guardia and make possible the creation of a partisan army. Efforts to resolve these differences failed and, until they withdrew, the Marines continued to operate as if the original agreement was in effect.

Meanwhile, Mondaca persisted in efforts to manipulate the force for his own political interests. In April 1929, he ordered the Guardia to arrest sixteen of his political opponents, including a prominent newspaper editor. The State Department opposed such action, placing the Guardia in an awkward position. As the police force, it was supposed to carry out arrest orders from the courts, but, since the President controlled these, involvement in political arrests became virtually inevitable. In May, Moncada ordered the arrest of over forty more political opponents. Again, the State Department protested, but to no avail.[27]

The Nicaraguan court system was a constant problem for the Marines and the Guardia. In Haiti and in the Dominican Republic, Americans had exercised some control over the courts, but not in Nicaragua. There existed a welter of local and national tribunals, often with unclear and overlapping jurisdictions, and all highly politicized.[28] For either personal or political motives, judges often refused to try or sentence individuals brought before them by the Guardia. In rural areas, Guardia officers sometimes resorted to holding court themselves, trying everything from homicides to civil cases to domestic disputes, but this was not the general rule and the court system remained an object of constant frustration.[29]

Other disputes between Moncada and the Americans involved the Guardia's budget. The onset of the great depression had created serious financial problems for both governments, but Moncada saw in these more opportunities to extend his control over military affairs. In 1929, he tried to reduce the Guardia's budget to $800,000, an amount that would have forced a sharp reduction in personnel, and might have opened a door for the return of the "volunteer" army. The newly appointed American Minister, Matthew Hanna, an Army veteran who had served in Cuba, tried to compromise. He suggested that municipal police, paid by local communities, should take over much of the police duties, freeing the Guard to focus on the fight with Sandino. The State Department rejected this idea, insisting that the Guardia remain Nicaragua's only police as well as military force. The following year Moncada tried to force Marines serving with the Guardia to take a 20-percent pay cut, something they, not surprisingly, resisted.[30] They denounced this effort as:

> . . . only one cog in the policy to destroy the Guardia. Without asking that the United States withdraw the Marines attached to the Guardia he kills it by non-support and thus lays the blame for the death on the United States and attains his own end: that of substituting Nicaraguans of his own personal choice for United States Marines.[31]

Escalated attacks by Sandino cooled this dispute as conditions made it imperative that the Guardia expand, not contract. When the Marines turned over command at the end of 1932 it had reached a total strength of 267 officers and 2,240 enlisted men.[32] In addition, due to President Moncada's efforts, there were several hundred municipal police, ostensibly under Guardia control, but recruited locally and paid for by liquor taxes. Another group, known as civicos, served as both a reserve force and as private guards for companies and farms. Finally, beginning in 1931, a force of 300 auxiliares was created, short-term armed groups who accompanied the Guardia on specific missions. Another 250 were added in 1932 and these sometimes operated independently. In all cases, Guardia officers, supplied through the Guardia's Quartermaster Department, and, at least in theory, subject to Guardia regulations, commanded the auxiliares.[33] They do not seem to have generated the controversy engendered by the earlier voluntaries and, in early 1933, after peace was negotiated with Sandino, they were apparently disbanded.

Despite limited funds, constant combat, and seemingly endless political disputes, the Marines did a reasonably good job in organizing and training the Guardia. While under their command it remained nonpartisan, reasonably honest, and by far the best trained, disciplined, and equipped force in Nicaraguan history. The very nature of Marine leadership and training, however, contributed to future problems in the nation's civil-military relations. As one scholar has noted that, "despite [the Marines] efforts to eradicate the old caudillo style military history of Nicaragua

[they] ended up recreating the same style of command within the new Guardia."[34]

The problem was what is characterized in Spanish as personalismo, the habit, especially among Latin American militaries, of giving prime loyalty not to a nation or an institution, but to one's immediate commander. It is common to address a superior officer as mi General or mi Capitan, my General or Captain, emphasizing the highly personal nature of the relationship. This had always been a dominant characteristic in Nicaragua, and troops reacted to Marine officers much as they had to earlier Nicaraguan leaders. As Marine Lieutenant Colonel Arthur Racicot noted in 1930:

> The morale of the Guardia Nacional is in general satisfactory. Their loyalty appears almost wholly based on personal loyalty to their officers. Development of loyalty to their government as the duty of a soldier, above everything else, is not apparent in any perceptible degree, yet.[35]

Writing after the Marines withdrew another officer stressed the role of personal loyalties in effective command of Guardia units, emphasizing that, "The Marine became guide, philosopher, and friend, and, in most instances, the idol of his command." He concluded that, "with a careful eye upon their comfort and wellbeing, kindness, and an occasional word of appreciation and the Jefe became the demigod of his men.[36]

An exacerbating factor was the series of disputes between the Marines and Nicaraguan politicians. Many Guardia officers made little effort to conceal their contempt for the entire political class. One senior officer went so far as to declare that, "most Nicaraguan politicians should be in jail."[37] Such open contempt did nothing to promote Guardia loyalty to the government. Instead, both the Nicaraguan officers and enlisted men increasingly came to think of themselves as a class apart, not just separate from, but in most ways superior, to the political leadership. At its most extreme, this attitude created the image that they were the true defenders of the state and politicians among the principal menaces.

Racial, religious, and cultural prejudices also hampered the development of the Guardia, though to a lesser extent than was the case in Haiti or the Dominican Republic. It must again be recalled that such prejudices were extremely common in the United States at this time. The Corps had no minority officers or enlisted men and many came from the segregated South. In addition, anti-Catholic sentiment was common, reflected in the defeat of Al Smith's run for the presidency in 1928. What is notable is the extent to which many Marines, detailed to the Guardia, were able to overcome or at least modify their prejudices. Compliments on the quality of Nicaraguan troops were frequent and at times those of mixed heritage were seen as superior to the more Europeanized elites. At the same time, many of the enlisted men may have found the class prejudices of their American officers less intense than those they had experienced under Nicaraguan command. In the Marine Corps, ties between officers and enlisted personnel, especially the famous Gunnery Sergeants, were always close and this attitude carried over to their development of the Guardia. One prejudice, however, did have a real impact. As in Haiti, the Marines were never willing to have a native officer in a position of command over any Marine. This insured that Nicaraguans did not fill any posts above the rank of Captain until just before the final withdrawal. The lack of any professional preparation of the higher officer corps would create major problems for the future of the Guardia and of Nicaragua.

Sandino was not the only major challenge that the Guardia confronted. On 31 March 1931, a powerful earthquake devastated the city of Managua. Damage and casualties were immense, water and electricity services were disrupted, and fires broke out, destroying much of what the earthquake had spared.[38] The Guardia's Marine Commander immediately declared martial law, and his troops and the members of the Marine Brigade in Managua worked furiously to stem the fires and prevent looting. They also took over efforts to provide food, water, and medical care for the city's surviving inhabitants. Almost all the buildings used by the Guardia were destroyed, as was the National Penitentiary.[39] Despite immense difficulties, the force functioned well and probably did more to enhance its image by these actions than at any other time. In December 1972, when an earthquake again devastated Managua, the Guardia's performance would produce condemnation rather than praise.

By the time of the earthquake, preparations were already underway for transferring command to Nicaraguan officers and withdrawing the Marines. President Hoover's desire to end American military interventions in Latin America, budgetary pressures exacerbated by the depression, and Secretary of State Stimson's belief that the interventions hampered his efforts to oppose Japan's invasion of Manchuria all added to the urgency. In April 1930, a Nicaraguan military academy was finally opened, but there were only nine students in the initial class. Increased clashes with Sandino's forces led to a very premature graduation of this class, but this still left the Guard with only 15 Nicaraguans among the 220 officers.[40] A class of thirty-seven, four of whom were already Guardia officers, was admitted to the military academy in November 1930 and twenty-seven graduated on 1 June 1931. The following class graduated fifty-nine new second lieutenants in April 1932. Admissions to each class were supposed to be nonpartisan, but President Moncada had to approve them and he clearly favored those with Liberal party connections.[41]

The State Department continued efforts to limit political influences, but with little success. Washington was determined to end the intervention when the victor in the 1932 presidential elections took office and pressures to comply with this mandate overwhelmed all other concerns. The Academy would produce enough graduates to fill all the slots for second lieutenants, and promotions of existing offices would take care of the positions for first lieutenants and some of those for captains. But there was no provision for filling the higher ranks. These positions would be critical in determining the Guard's trajectory once the Marines departed.

Washington did not seem to take serious notice of this problem until February 1932. Laurence Duggan of the State Department's Division of Latin American Affairs wrote a memo noting that the Guardia had no regular promotion procedures and no means of preventing the President "from appointing to all the high commands his own henchmen, pledged to carry out his personal or party wishes."[42] The State Department then asked its Nicaraguan Legation to report on preparations for turning over command. Chargé Willard Beaulac responded by forwarding a November 1931 proposal by Guardia Jefe Director, General Calvin B. Matthews, that Nicaragua adopt a law freeing the Guardia from local political control and prohibiting its members from any political participation including voting. He also included a later message from Matthews noting that none of the Academy graduates would have the experience necessary for high command and that these posts would need to be filled by "Nicaraguans of mature age and with previous military experience," who would be appointed by the winner of the 1932 elections.[43] Since the only way Nicaraguans outside of the Guardia had gained such experience was in bitterly partisan civil conflicts, this made the future of the concept of a nonpartisan constabulary dubious at best.

Washington's response to this situation seems to have been a combination of denial and wishful thinking. On 17 May 1932, Acting Secretary of State Francis White wrote Matthew Hanna, the American Minister in Nicaragua:

> It is going to be difficult to maintain the theory of the
> Guardia as a nonpartisan organization if outsiders are
> appointed to high command. However, in view of the fact

110

that no Nicaraguans have so far been trained to hold grades higher than that of lieutenant, I suppose it may be necessary to go outside of the Guardia for some of the appointments to higher grades. It would of course be advisable if such appointments could be given to Nicaraguans who do not have a record of strong political partisanship.[44]

In June 1932, Matthews pointed out that appointments to higher positions could precipitate a conflict between the incumbent and incoming presidents and therefore urged Washington to allow fifty Marine officers to stay for an additional two months to facilitate the turnover. Secretary of State Stimson firmly rejected this suggestion.[45] An alternate plan, proposed by Matthews, was accepted by the State Department. It provided that each major party candidate for president should prepare a list of officers, drawn equally from both parties, before the election and that President Moncada should agree to appoint the list of the winning candidate. However, the key post of Jefe Director, was exempted from this and would obviously be a supporter of the winning candidate and his party. The Acting Secretary of State seemed satisfied with this arrangement, declaring that it provided for "continuance of the nonpartisan nature of the Guardia since its officers will be drawn equally from the two historic political parties."[46] This assertion was patently false, since the new officers would be appointed because of their political loyalties, not the lack thereof. Moreover, the Jefe Director would almost certainly be an individual of strong political loyalties and would have great control over future assignments and promotions, virtually assuring that the force would become increasingly partisan.

With no better options readily available, this plan was put in motion. At President Moncada's suggestion, the two major presidential candidates, on the day before the election, signed an agreement, pledging to keep the Guardia nonpartisan and to give President Moncada, in agreement with General Matthews, the right to appoint the officers on the winning candidates list.[47] On 6 November, the elections were held, under American supervision, and the Liberal Party candidate, Dr. Juan Bautista Sacasa, won a decisive victory. The Guardia performed well during the elections and even the defeated party acknowledged that it had remained completely neutral.

While Sacasa supposedly was free to appoint whomever he wished as the Guardia's new Jefe Director, he had to negotiate this with both President Moncada and the American Minister, Matthew Hanna. A letter from Matthews to Moncada confirmed this, saying Sacasa had been given three names—Anastasio Somoza García, Gustavo Abaunza, and José María Zelaya—from which to choose the "higher officials."[48] All three were strong partisans of Moncada's faction of the Liberal Party. Eventually Somoza was made Jefe Director, and Abaunza Chief of Staff.[49]

Sacasa found Somoza, Moncada's acting Foreign Minister, the least objectionable of this group, largely because he was married to the incoming President's niece. The Americans wanted him because he had long worked with them, often serving as a buffer between the volatile and frequently intoxicated Moncada and American diplomatic and military officials. He also had studied at the Pierce School of Accounting in Philadelphia where he learned English and became an ardent baseball fan. Hanna had openly stated his preference for Somoza, characterizing him as "the best man in the country for the position" and concluding, "no one will labor as intelligently or conscientiously to maintain the nonpartisan character of the Guardia or will be as efficient in all matters connected with the administration and command of the Force."[50]

With this obstacle removed the Marines set about making final preparations for the change of command and their departure. Matthews and his staff prepared a large number of proposed laws governing the Guardia that they wanted adopted, but no Nicaraguan administration ever acted on these. On 1 January 1933, Matthews turned over command to Somoza and departed in such a rush that his Chief of Staff doubted that he even finished packing.[51] They left behind the best trained, armed, and equipped military force in Nicaragua's history. Despite limited academic preparation, the junior officers were better trained than any previous officer corps and in addition most had some combat experience, often under Marine direction. Separate medical, quartermaster, and communications departments were organized and functioning.

The majority of the Guardia were destined to function more as police than as military, and in this area, too, the force was better trained and disciplined than ever before, with much of the petty graft and almost all of the political harassment previously characteristic of Nicaraguan police eliminated. On most technical matters, the Marines had done as good a job as possible under the circumstances. The chances of these changes enduring would now depend on Nicaraguan leadership. That leadership, it soon became apparent, was determined to mold the Guardia into an instrument of personal ambitions.

Some individuals in both the State Department and the Marine Corps had a good idea of what the future was likely to hold. Laurence Duggan, ever the pessimistic realist, had, as early as November 1931, noted that the animosity between traditional parties probably made establishing a nonpartisan constabulary an impossibility, and openly wondered what had ever made American officials think that might be possible.[52] The following year Duggan was even more pessimistic, predicting:

> Upon the withdrawal of the Marine officer in the Guardia next fall the forces of disintegration will be set into action. . . . It is a foregone conclusion that Nicaragua will not maintain the Guardia along present Marine Corps lines. The loss of the spirit of impartial service, so laboriously instilled, involves a return to a partisan, political constabulary. Judging from the historical position of the Army in Central America and more particularly in Nicaragua a strictly nonpartisan military is not, at the present time, a possibility.[53]

Many of the Marines who had served with the Guardia were also pessimistic about its future. Writing in the November 1932 issue of the Marine Corps Gazette, Lieutenant Colonel Robert Denig, who had served as Guardia Chief of Staff until injuries suffered in the 1931 earthquake forced his evacuation, criticized the plan for political appointments to the Guardia's higher positions, and concluded, "At best there is sure to be a shakeup in the Guardia; it will soon become a partisan force used to further the party in power."[54] Even General Matthews, the Guardia's last American commander, was pessimistic, admitting that the best that could be hoped would be that the politically appointed officers would have a minimum, not an absence of political bias, and noting that political bias already existed as Moncada had openly favored Liberals for both officer and enlisted positions.[55]

These fears would prove all too true. At first, though, it seemed as if the Marine's withdrawal might bring peace to Nicaragua. Sandino had often declared that he would quit fighting when the Marines left and to the surprise of many, he kept his promise. On 23 January, a fifteen-day truce was declared to allow negotiations, and, in early February, Sacasa and Sandino agreed to a treaty that provided for an end to the fighting, a general amnesty, and the disarmament of all but 100 of Sandino's men.

This agreement may have come just in time for General Somoza and the Guardia. The political appointments to the senior officer positions angered some military academy graduates and a disgruntled group plotted to force the president to fire all but Somoza and promote junior officers in their place. The plot was discovered, but, unsure of its dimensions, the president and his Jefe Director simply reassigned the ringleaders to remote posts or administrative billets.[56]

Guardia unity was restored more by a common dislike of the peace terms obtained by Sandino than by anything else. The former insurgent leader's retention of his own armed force, in contravention of the stipulation that the Guardia, was to be the nation's sole armed force, was the greatest issue. Somoza repeatedly asked the American Minister, Arthur Bliss Lane, for permission to "lock Sandino up," an action Lane always refused to endorse.[57] But, pressured by the Guardia's officer corps, Somoza decided to move ahead anyway. On the night of 21 February 1934, Sandino was seized as he left a meeting with President Sacasa and, along with several of his chief lieutenants, shot. At the same time, other Guardia units attacked his followers camped along the Coco River.[58]

At first terrified that Sacasa might seize on the killings as an excuse to replace him, Somoza quickly recovered his nerve when the president failed to act. He now began to maneuver, first to gain complete control over the Guardia then to make himself president. The first step was having the congress pass an override of a presidential veto of a general amnesty for all those involved in Sandino's murder.[59] Somoza also had to put down several plots against him from within the Guardia during 1934 and 1935. Their failure helped the Jefe Director to steadily purge the force of officers whose loyalty was suspect. In the process most of the Conservatives who had been appointed to senior positions following the 1932 election were forced out.

With the Guardia now largely loyal to him, Somoza put into action plans to make himself president. President Sacasa attempted to block his ambitions, but to no avail. In June 1936, there was a brief armed confrontation between the Guardia and Sacasa's supporters. The President appealed to the United States and other nations for support, but beyond a few verbal statements, got nothing. Terrified for his own safety, he ordered his supporters to surrender, then resigned and fled the country.[60] With Sacasa out of the way, the Liberal Party obediently nominated Somoza for president, the opposition boycotted the 1936 elections, and he was declared the victor with over 99 percent of the votes. As the Constitution required, Somoza ostensibly stepped down as Jefe Director during the campaign, but shortly after his victory resumed the post, combining in his person the civilian and military leadership of the nation.[61]

What many had feared had come to pass. The Guardia had become not only an instrument of partisan politics, it had essentially taken over politics, dominating the Liberal Party, intimidating the opposition, and placing its commander in the presidency. This came as no surprise to Arthur Bliss Lane, who a year earlier had written:

The people who created the G.N. had no adequate understanding of the psychology of the people here. Otherwise they would not have bequeathed Nicaragua with an instrument to blast constitutional procedure off the map. Did it ever occur to the eminent statesmen who created the G.N. that personal ambition lurks in the human breast, even in Nicaragua. In my opinion it is one of the sorriest examples on our part of our inability to understand that we should not meddle in other peoples affairs.[62]

For the next 33 years, the history of Nicaragua, the Guardia Nacional, and the Somoza family were inextricably intertwined. Anastasio Somoza García and his sons built their power on the twin pillars of control of the Guardia and maintaining the image of Washington's support. In the process, they constantly strove to portray all opposition as either pro-Axis (through 1945) or pro-Communist.[63] They became a constant ally of the United States, promptly declaring war on Japan and Germany in 1941, always voting with Washington in the United Nations, sending his sons, Luis and Anastasio Somoza Debayle, to study in the United States (Luis graduated from Louisiana State and Anastasio from West Point) and even naming Managua's main street Avenida Roosevelt. In return, the United States provided training and military assistance to the Guardia, especially during World War II and following Castro's assumption of power in Cuba. When the CIA wanted bases to train an exile army to oust left-leaning Jacobo Árbenz from power in Guatemala, Somoza readily complied.[64] In return, Nicaragua received generous amounts of American military assistance and training and the Guardia's strength steadily expanded.[65] His sons later supplied the bases from which the CIA launched its unsuccessful Cuban invasion in 1961.[66] This contributed to an intense hatred between the two regimes and to Castro's strong support for the Nicaraguan insurgents of the FSLN.

Relations were not always smooth. After World War II, the Truman administration pressured Somoza not to run for re-election, and then, when he overthrew his handpicked successor withdrew recognition, ended military training and assistance for a time. The Eisenhower administration helped block his efforts to overthrow the Costa Rican government in 1954.[67] Despite Nicaraguan support at the Bay of Pigs, the Kennedy administration tried to pressure the sons to lessen their grip on power, but only succeeded in having a puppet president installed for one term. In every case, security considerations, the identification of the regimes opponents with Communism and, eventually, with Castro, and the perceived lack of viable alternatives aborted these efforts and enabled the Somozas to maintain their power and the Guardia to continue receiving US assistance and training. They took full advantage of every such opportunity and, until relations broke down in 1978, under the Carter administration, sent more individuals to the US Army's School of the Americas in the Canal Zone than any other Latin American nation.[68]

Anastasio Somoza García was assassinated in 1956, but his sons Luis and Anastasio (Tachito) Somoza Debayle quickly assumed power. Luis handled politics and Anastasio commanded the Guardia until Luis died in 1967. The younger brother then tried to direct both political and military affairs, plus manage the family's huge business interests, but lacked the skills of his father and brother. Corruption became more and more blatant, and frustrated youth increasingly turned to the Cuban-backed Sandinista guerrillas. Relations with the Roman Catholic Church were also deteriorating as Guardia human rights violations increased. When the Guardia largely disintegrated following the 1972 earthquake and Tachito used the event to further enrich himself opposition within the business class mounted as well.[69]

The regime's final collapse began in January 1978 with the assassination of Somoza's most prominent political opponent, newspaper editor Pedro Joaquín Chamorro. Widespread strikes quickly followed and there were scattered uprisings that the Guardia crushed. Relations with the United States deteriorated and Venezuela, Panama, and Costa Rica took the lead among Latin American nations in calling for Somoza's ouster. In August, an FSLN commando unit, led by Edén Pastora (Commandante Zero) infiltrated Managua and took the Congress hostage. Despite opposition from elements of the Guardia, Somoza Debayle negotiated a settlement. Political prisoners were released, an FSLN communiqué was broadcast on radio and television, and the guerrillas were flown to safety in Panama and Venezuela.[70] This inspired a rash of uprisings across Nicaragua that the Guardia again put down, this time with greatly increased brutality, including bombing civilian areas and shooting any young men suspected of Sandinista sympathies.[71]

The United States devoted the next several months to trying to leverage the Somozas out of power, but to no avail. Military assistance and training were suspended, but the regime managed to find other sources, including Israel and rightwing Latin American governments. In May 1979, the FSLN launched coordinated attacks on the regime from within Nicaragua and from Costa Rica. Frantic US efforts to negotiate an end to the fighting, including efforts to get the Organization of American States to intervene, and to negotiate the survival of at least elements of the Guardia failed.[72] Somoza was finally persuaded to resign in July 1979 and the remnants of the Guardia fled into exile or sought refuge with the Red Cross in Managua. This sanctuary was quickly violated and most of the officers and enlisted men from combat units were imprisoned. The United States created Guardia Nacional de Nicaragua had ceased to exist.[73]

The Nicaraguan experience demonstrates again that, while technical expertise can be created, altering political behavior and institutions are much more difficult, if not impossible. It also underscores the reality that policies towards small, weak nations are so often overtaken by perceived wider concerns, be they developing a nonintervention policy, fighting global enemies, promoting democracy and human rights, or simply wanting stability at almost any price in order not to have attention diverted from more pressing matters. In the end, neither stability nor wider interests were achieved and, during the 1980s, the United States would find itself once more absorbed with trying to deal with Nicaragua.

Notes

1. For details on this period, see Dana Gardner Munro, *Intervention and Dollar Diplomacy in the Caribbean, 1900–1921* (Princeton, NJ: Princeton University Press, 1964), 160–216.
2. Richard L. Millett, *Guardians of the Dynasty: A History of the US Created Guardia Nacional de Nicaragua and the Somoza Family* (Maryknoll, NY: Orbis Books, 1977), 34–35.
3. Thomas M. Leonard, *US Policy and Arms Limitation in Central America: The Washington Conference of 1923* (Los Angeles, CA: Center for the Study of Armament and Disarmament, California State University, Los Angeles, 1982), 59 and 67.
4. Leonard, 13–14.
5. Ibid., 35–36.
6. Walter Thurston to Secretary of State Kellogg, 15 May 1925, *Papers Relating to Foreign Relations of the United States*, Vol. II (1925), 628–630.
7. Major Calvin B. Carter to US Minister Charles Eberhardt, 30 September 1925, RG 59, 817.1051/87 (enclosure).
8. Eberhardt to Kellogg, 3 November 1925, RG 59,817.1051/88.
9. Millett, *Guardians*, 45–47.
10. Eberhardt to Kellogg, 14 March 1926, RG 59, 817.1051/98.
11. Eberhardt to Kellogg, 8 April 1926, RG 59, 817.1051/99.
12. For details of Stimson's mission and his agreement with General Moncada, see Henry L. Stimson, *American Policy in Nicaragua* (New York, NY: Charles Scribner's Sons, 1927). This was republished in 1991 with additional essays by Paul Boeker, Alan Brinkley and Andres Perez plus the inclusion of a State Department History of US–Nicaraguan Relations from 1909 to 1932 under the title *Henry L. Stimson's American Policy in Nicaragua* (New York, NY: Markus Wiener Publishing, Inc., 1992).
13. Millett, *Guardians*, 61.
14. Quoted in Neill Macaulay, *The Sandino Affair* (Chicago, IL: Quadrangle Books, 1967), 70.
15. For the best description of these events and of the subsequent over five years of war between Sandino and the Guard and the Marines, see Macaulay.
16. Captain Herbert S. Keimling to Major Fleming, 11 March 1933, RG 127, Entry 198, Papers of the *Jefe Director of the Guardia Nacional de Nicaragua*.
17. Millett, *Guardians*, 74.
18. For a more detailed description of these disputes, see Millett, *Guardians*, 68–70.
19. "Agreement between the United States and Nicaragua Establishing the Guardia Nacional de Nicaragua," 22 December 1927, *Papers Relating to Foreign Relations of the United States*, Vol. III (1927), 434–439.
20. Millett, *Guardians*, 71 and 77.
21. Julian C. Smith et al., *A Review of the Organization and Operations of the Guardia Nacional de Nicaragua*, US Marine Corps Headquarters, nd.,

302–407; Richard Grossman, "Hermanos de la Patria: Nationalism, Honor and Rebellion: Augusto Sandino and the Army in Defense of the National Sovereignty of Nicaragua, 1927–1934," (Ph.D. dissertation, University of Chicago, 1996), 198.

22. One of these assistants was Army Captain Matthew B. Ridgeway.

23. Admiral David Foote Sellers to Admiral Hughes, n.d., Papers of Admiral David Foote Sellers, Naval Historical Foundation Collection, Manuscript Division, Library of Congress, Box 3.

24. Sellers to Admiral Hughes, Papers of Admiral David Foote Sellers, Box 3.

25. Macaulay, 136–144.

26. Secretary of State Stimson to the American Minister in Nicaragua, Matthew Hanna, 29 May 1929, *Papers Relating to Foreign Relations of the United States*, Vol. III (1929), 629–633.

27. US Minister to Nicaragua, Matthew B. Hanna, to Stimson, 9 September 1929, *Papers Relating to Foreign Relations of the United States,* Vol. III (1929), 596–601; US Minister to Nicaragua, Matthew B. Hanna, to Stimson, 19 September 1929, *Papers Relating to Foreign Relations of the United States,* Vol. III (1929), 596–601; US Minister to Nicaragua, Matthew B. Hanna, to Stimson, 25 September 1929, *Papers Relating to Foreign Relations of the United States,* Vol.e III (1929), 596–601; US Minister to Nicaragua, Matthew B. Hanna, to Stimson, 29 September 1929, *Papers Relating to Foreign Relations of the United States,* Vol. III (1929), 596–601; Francis White to Hanna, 29 November 1929, *Papers Relating to Foreign Relations of the United States*, Vol. III (1929), 609.

28. Smith et al., 45–46.

29. Captain Evans F. Carlson, "The Guardia as a Police Force," *Leatherneck*, Vol. XV (October 1932), 20 and 62.

30. Millett, *Guardians*, 114–115.

31. Unsigned, undated memorandum from Headquarters, US Marine Corps Adjutant and Inspectors General Correspondence, RG 127.

32. Smith et al., 16.

33. Ibid., 16–19.

34. Grossman, 185.

35. Quoted in Grossman, 211.

36. Colonel H. C. Reisinger, "*La Palabra del Gringo,* Leadership of the Nicaraguan National Guard," *United States Naval Institute Proceedings*, Vol. LXI (February 1935), 216 and 217.

37. Quoted in Grossman.

38. For a description of the earthquake and the resulting damage, see Gustavo Tijerino, *El terremoto mas barbaro de la historia*, Vol. I (Leon, Nicaragua: Instituto Technico La Salle de Leon, 1973), 25–32.

39. Smith et al., 123–134.

40. Millett, *Guardians*, 126.

41. Hanna to Stimson, 11 December 1930, RG 59, 817.223/2. Nicaraguan politics were sharply divided along family and regional lines and it was relatively easy to determine political preferences.

42. Memorandum from Laurence Duggan to Edmund Wilson, 25 February 1932, RG 59, 817.1051/611.

43. General Matthews to Beaulac, 16 November 1931 and 4 April 1931, *Papers Relating to Foreign Relations of the United States*, Vol. V (1932), 855–858.

44. Francis White to Matthew Hanna, 17 April 1932, RG 59, 817.1051/643.

45. Millett, *Guardians*, 129.

46. Acting Secretary of State Castle to Hanna, 30 August 1932, *Papers Relating to Foreign Relations of the United States*, Vol. V (1932), 871–872.

47. "Agreement Signed on November 5, 1932, Providing for the Maintenance of the Non-Partisan Character of the Guardia Nacional de Nicaragua," *Papers Relating to Foreign Relations of the United States*, Vol. V (1932), 887.

48. Matthews to Moncada, 21 November 1932, Records of the Marine Corps in Nicaragua, Box 11, Marine Corps Historical Archives. When I examined these records in the 1960s they were located at the Marine Corps Archives in the Navy Yard, but have since been moved to the National Archives, and included in RG 127.

49. For a complete list of the forty-two political appointees to the officer corps, see Jorge Eduardo Arellano, *La Pax Americana en Nicaragua, 1910–1932* (Managua, Nicaragua: Academia de Geografía y Historia de Nicaragua, 2004), 277–278.

50. Hanna to White, 28 October 1932, RG 59, 817.1051//7011/2.

51. Interview with Lieutenant General Julian C. Smith, Arlington, VA, May 1964.

52. Memorandum by Duggan, 16 November 1931, RG 59, 711.17/253.

53. Memorandum from Duggan to Wilson, 23 March 1932, RG 59, 817.1051/643.

54. Lieutenant Colonel Robert L. Denig, "Native Officer Corps, Guardia Nacional de Nicaragua," *Marine Corps Gazette*, Vol. XVII (November 1932), 77.

55. Matthews to Hanna, 15 June 1932 and 8 August 1932, printed in Smith, 149 and 151–152.

56. Millett, *Guardians*, 145–146.

57. Arthur Bliss Lane to Josephus Daniels, 4 March 1934, Papers of Ambassador Arthur Bliss Lane, Manuscripts Division, Yale University Library, New Haven, CT.

58. Macaulay, 249–256.

59. Knut Walter, *The Regime of Anastasio Somoza, 1936–1956* (Chapel Hill, NC: The University of North Carolina Press, 1993), 34–35.

60. Millett, *Guardians*, 169–181. For President Sacasa's own account, see Juan Bautista Sacasa, *Comó y por qué caí del poder* (Third edition) (Managua, Nicaragua: Vanguardia, 1988).

61. Millett, *Guardians*, 181–182.

62. Lane to Beaulac, 27 July 1935, Papers of Ambassador Arthur Bliss Lane.

63. For a description of how Anastasio Somoza García held on to power, see Richard L. Millett, "Anastasio Somoza García, A Brief History of Nicaragua's

Enduring Dictator," *Revista/Review Interamericana*, Vol. VII, No. 3 (November 1932), 486–508.

64. For Nicaragua's role in the 1954 overthrow of Arbenz, see Piero Gleijeses, *Shattered Hope: The Guatemalan Revolution and the United States, 1944–1954* (Princeton, NJ: Princeton University Press, 1991), 110–113, 241–242, 248–251, 265–266, 291–293.

65. Walter, 214.

66. For Nicaragua's role, see Howard Jones, *The Bay of Pigs* (New York, NY: Oxford University Press, 2008), 73–74, 88–89, 96.

67. For details on the feud between the Somozas and President José Figueres of Costa Rica, see Charles Ameringer, *Don Pepe: A Political Biography of José Figueres of Costa Rica* (Albuquerque, NM: University of New Mexico Press, 1978), 76–83 and 119–120.

68. Millett, *Guardians*, 252.

69. Ibid., *Guardians*, 235–239,

70. For a description of this, see Bernard Diedrich, *Somoza and the Legacy of US Involvement in Central America* (New York, NY: E.P. Dutton, 1981), 176–188.

71. Robert Kagan, *A Twilight Struggle: American Power and Nicaragua, 1977–1990* (New York, NY: The Free Press, 1996), 58–59.

72. For insider descriptions of US efforts to resolve the conflict and of Somoza's fall, see Robert A. Pastor, *Condemned to Repetition: The United States and Nicaragua* (Princeton, NJ: Princeton University Press, 1987); Anthony Lake, *Somoza Falling: The Nicaraguan Dilemma: A Portrait of Washington at Work* (Boston, MA: Houghton Mifflin, 1989); Lawrence Pezullo and Ralph Pezullo, *At the Fall of Somoza* (Pittsburgh, PA: University of Pittsburgh Press, 1993). For a Sandinista account, see General Humberto Ortega Saavedra, *La Epopeya de la Insurrección* (Managua, Nicaragua: LEA Grupo Editorial, 2004).

73. For a discussion of Nicaragua's military under the Sandinistas, see Luis Humberto Guzmán, "Nicaragua's Armed Forces: An Assessment of Their Political Power," in Richard L. Millett and Michael Gold-Biss, eds., *Beyond Praetorianism: The Latin American Military in Transition* (Miami, FL: North-South Center Press, University of Miami, 1996), 157–180.

Chapter 8

Conclusions: Lessons Lost and Lessons Forgotten

A hundred and ten years after the United States began developing the Constabulary in the Philippines and the Rural Guard in Cuba, it finds itself again engaged in efforts to create security forces, this time in Iraq and Afghanistan. The problems of ethnic divisions, active insurgencies, limited resources, language and cultural barriers, and seemingly endless political conflicts which bedeviled efforts to create security forces in the first third of the 20th century all seem to be reoccurring in the first decade of the 21st. As Yogi Berra has observed, "it's déjà vu all over again." The question is, can we learn from the problems of the past and achieve better results in the future?

The US efforts to create constabulary-type forces in the first third of the 20th century produced disappointing results. Every one of the six nations involved—the Philippines, Cuba, Panama, Haiti, the Dominican Republic, and Nicaragua—ultimately fell under dictatorial rule. In all but the Philippines, control over the military brought these regimes to power and sustained them. In the Philippines, the military, including the constabulary, initially supported the Marcos dictatorship, but ultimately split and the constabulary was an important element in the uprising that finally forced him from power. In every case but the Philippines, the United States found itself intervening again, either with regular military force (in the Dominican Republic, Haiti, Panama) or with proxy forces (in Cuba and Nicaragua).

Also disturbing is the fate of these forces. In Cuba, the Rural Guard and its descendents were essentially destroyed three times, first when the Guard lost its independence and became an adjunct of the army, second when the officer corps was destroyed in the sergeants' revolt, and finally when the entire military apparatus was eliminated by Fidel Castro. In Panama, the force became progressively more militarized and more corrupt, culminating in the Noriega dictatorship. It took another US intervention to oust this regime and in the process the military was destroyed. In Haiti, the military made and unmade presidents until Duvalier created his own paramilitary thugs, the *Tonton Macoute*, to neutralize the Army. After Duvalier, the military returned to its old habits until a US-led intervention ended its existence. In the Dominican Republic, by contrast, the 1965 US intervention may have prevented the Army's destruction while in Nicaragua the *Guardia Nacional* first became a tool of the Somoza family, and then was destroyed by Marxist guerrillas.

What can we learn from this unhappy history? Would a different US policy, altered goals and/or methods, have produced a fundamentally different result? To what extent was the United States the cause of their subsequent trajectories, and to what extent was this largely a likely, if not inevitable, result of each nation's history and social structure? When dealing with security forces in other nations, especially when there are major differences of power, culture, and human development, what are the limits of influence? The answers to such questions will always be at least partially speculative, but by raising these issues some fundamental principles can emerge.

Andrew Bacevich has observed that, "Good intentions detached from prudential considerations can easily lead to enormous mischief, both practical and moral."[1] This applies to some of Washington's efforts to create constabulary forces. The weakness, corruption, and repressive nature of traditional military forces in Haiti, the Dominican Republic, and Nicaragua were all too apparent. So too was their inability to control insurrections. But, when policies were being formulated, no American official, civilian or military, appears to have asked if replacing such forces with a better trained and equipped constabulary would change their relation to the rest of society or in any way alter the traditional political equation which made force the final arbiter. Nor does there appear to have been any questioning of how nationalist sentiments would react to a foreign-created security force, or how that force, itself, would react once foreign control was ended. Comparisons to colonial experiences, whether that of the United States in the Philippines or, as was often cited, that of the British in Egypt and India, was misleading as in those cases there was no prospect, at least in the foreseeable future, of constabularies coming under national control.

Instead of asking such questions, policymakers seem to have assumed that a constabulary created with American instructors and under American-imposed regulations would behave like an American military force. There was no understanding of traditional Latin American distinctions between state, government and population, with the military owing its allegiance only to the first of these and assuming the right to define when the government or the population became a threat to the state. Neither did there seem to be comprehension of the great gap between American and Latin political culture over the source and nature of citizens' rights. In the United States, rights were inherent and the state had only the power that its citizens gave it. In Latin America, citizens had only the rights the state allowed them and, if the state believed itself threatened, it could usually impose a state of siege that suspended all rights. This was compounded by Latin America's lack of a strong tradition of judicial independence. Courts were largely seen as an instrument of executive power and were designed principally to maintain order, not protect citizens' rights. Under such circumstances, a more efficient police usually meant a more repressive state, not more citizen security.[2]

None of this should be taken to mean that leaving the old military and police as they were offered any solution for American policy aims or for domestic peace and development. Abstaining from any effort to create effective security forces can produce its own version of policy disaster, as the American experiences in Lebanon and Somalia demonstrate. The issues in each case are less what can be done than what should not be done, and what are the likely unintended consequences of any program.

Analysis of these case studies can produce some basic principles. The first is the need for clarity of purpose. Simply wanting to create a constabulary force is not enough. There must be thought given to how this relates to other elements of government such as the courts, local governments, and treasury. A nation's internal divisions, racial, ethnic, religious, ideological and/or regional must be carefully taken into account in determining both personnel and mission. What exactly such a force can accomplish and how it is likely to evolve when left to its own devices should enter into planning at the earliest stages.

Second, there must be unity of effort. The bitter disputes between American civil and military personnel, notably, but, by no means exclusively in the Dominican Republic, are a case in point. They disrupted the effort to develop the *Guardia*, contributed to policy confusion in Washington, and ultimately made it more difficult for those on the scene to get a fair hearing for their concerns.

Third, goals must be realistic. A force created by outsiders, no matter how capable or dedicated, will be shaped by its domestic context. To the extent that it becomes a foreign transplant it will lose credibility, contribute to internal divisions, and become an object of nationalist attacks. Americans can train, equip, even command such forces, but in the end they will fall under national authority that will strive to remove all evidence of external domination.

This relates directly to the fourth and final basic point: know and accept the limits of influence. No matter what is done to mold and indoctrinate a foreign security force it will evolve into something different. No matter what efforts are made to shape attitudes towards civil authority, citizens' rights and legal responsibilities, post occupation realities will reshape if not eliminate such principles. This is not our country and everyone who is recruited into forces we create knows that and acts accordingly.

In addition to these broad principles, there are some specific lessons that can be drawn from these experiences and, hopefully, applied to present and possible future operations.[3]

1. You will have neither the time nor the resources necessary to do the job the way it should be done. Resources are always limited, newer problems always divert attention, political and popular support is a limited and diminishing resource. Arguing for more time, more resources can become a self-defeating exercise, diminishing credibility and diverting attention from determining urgent priorities.

2. Once national policy begins to focus on withdrawal, this concern will overwhelm all others. Anything that interferes with this goal will be shoved aside.

3. Always remember, technology transfers, values do not. It is relatively easy to train someone how to use a weapon; it is much more difficult to control when they use the weapon and against whom. Americans are very good at technical training and it is easy to measure success in such terms. But the political results of such training depend on the when and against whom aspects.

4. Keep in mind that in the creation of security forces you are dealing with adults. Their values are already well formed and largely immutable. They know their political and social environment better than you and they know what it takes to survive and prosper in it. Any aspect of training which runs contrary to this will have little if any impact. If an alteration in traditional patterns is perceived as advancing their goals, it may be accepted and incorporated, but if it is perceived as largely advancing your goals or if it runs contrary to their cultural values it will be rejected. One Nicaraguan experience provides a graphic, if somewhat comical example of this. The rates of sexually transmitted diseases among enlisted personnel of the *Guardia* were extremely high and the usual lectures on health and morality had the usual lack of effect. So the Navy doctors and Corpsmen passed out prophylactics. While the enlisted personnel insisted they were using them, infection rates continued to climb. One doctor decided to investigate and discovered that they were indeed being used—to polish their boots before they went off to the brothels on payday.[4] Having highly polished boots was

a source of male pride in Nicaragua, using a prophylactic was not. They took American technology and adapted it to their values.

5. Never assume that the motives for someone joining a foreign created security force are the same as those that motivate Americans. There is usually some similarity at enlisted levels, individuals may join because they need a job or hope to gain a skill. For those becoming officers, however, the motives may be very different. This is especially true in nations with deep internal divisions. Candidates may seek to advance their own ethnic/racial/religious group and/or counter the interests of others. They may be motivated largely by hopes for social advancement, for opportunity for personal enrichment, or a means of enhancing family security. What Americans would define as patriotic motives, seeking to serve one's nation, may be present, but usually to a lesser degree and are often absent altogether.

6. Using the military in the role of police is always a bad idea, although not using them in such a role may be even worse. When Washington conceived of creating these constabularies the assumption was that combining police and military functions would serve numerous purposes: reducing expenses, giving the new force a credible mission, curbing political manipulation and limiting corruption. What it did in fact do was exacerbate the tendency to overly centralized authority, eliminating any police responsibility to local authorities. In practice, individuals were sometimes deliberately assigned to areas where they had no local ties in order to undercut the power of regional leaders. In other cases, the constabulary was barely present and in its place local paramilitary forces were raised, operating largely outside the rule of law. Those assigned to police duties were under military authority and their officers often graduated from the national military academy. But these were usually those of less ability and/or ambition (and often in practice with fewer moral scruples). In none of these nations was there a tradition of a primary police responsibility being protecting average citizens and once national control was established over the police, protecting average citizens fell off their priority list and traditional attitudes toward the population returned, if they had ever been absent. Order took precedence over justice, and protecting privilege, not citizens' rights, was the priority.

7. Career military are not ideal trainers for police. The military, especially in the early 20th century, placed a higher value on order

and discipline than did society as a whole and often tended to treat foreign populations in policing situations as a potential enemy. Admiral Robison's inquiry as to whether he should consider the Dominicans as enemies illustrates this.[5] Military trainers were sometimes well versed in the technical skills needed for police work, but not in the human relations required. This is not meant as a criticism of the military; no one would expect a career police officer to be the ideal trainer of a combat unit. But it does highlight an ongoing problem and explains why the first Marine commander of the Managua police should plead for the Marines to "get up a pamphlet on practical police work" and argue that, "it should be made part of the law course in the Marine Corps schools."[6]

8. In nations with only a constabulary force, it is the police units that will have most contact with the population and will determine popular attitudes towards the institution as a whole. When corrupt, brutal and/or repressive they often generate violent resistance to authority. For a centralized, military command, efficiency and the maintenance of a least the appearance of order are normally more important that the state of police/civilian relations. For police units in most of these constabulary forces, their relationship with overall command authority is more important and career promoting than their relations with the local authority or population. But for political stability and for countering an existing insurgency the opposite is true: relationships with local populations are key.

9. Efforts to change a society largely through changing its security forces never produce the desired effect and inevitably bring undesired effects. The most extreme case of this is when security forces are modernized, but the overall administration of justice is not. When police and judicial organs are in conflict, or when the courts simply don't function effectively two things invariably happen. The police increasingly take justice into their own hands, including eliminating prisoners, and corruption spreads hand-in-hand with rising police frustrations.[7]

10. Prejudices and stereotypes always hinder effective force development. They are never a secret from those who are being trained and can have significant, negative long-range results. The Haitian case is rife with examples, but this impacted to a greater or lesser extent on every one of the six cases included in this study. The worst example was the Trujillo court-martial in the Dominican Republic. By not expecting a Dominican officer to come close to the stan-

dards they set for themselves, the American officers of the *Guardia* helped advance the career of a future mass murderer. Taking into account cultural and educational differences does not equate with abandoning standards. Differences do not imply inferiority.[8]

11. Language skills and their cultural context are vital. This does not simply mean achieving a certain degree of fluency, being able to give training lectures and conduct drills. It means learning the values that a language carries. It means knowing that in Spanish there is no good translation for rule of law, that in most indigenous languages our concepts of justice and of the state protecting citizens' rights are largely absent. It means knowing why, for a Creole-speaking Haitian peasant, the concept of state authority and the phrase "to squeeze and suck" are essentially synonymous.[9] Language shapes relationships with authority, values and attitudes, loyalties and expectations. What you think you are saying and what they hear are never exactly the same and sometimes the differences can be critical.

12. Most of your influence will leave when you do. The traditions of national culture and the realities of existing power structures will rapidly replace most of whatever influence you may have had. This has nothing to do with whether you are liked or not, something to which Americans often give too much weight. It simply reflects who is in a position to dispense rewards and punishments, whose expectations one needs to meet.

13. Secondary issues in development and training often become major issues once command is transferred. The role of intelligence is a key example. Under American control intelligence functioned largely as a tactical tool for both the police and the military. Data collection and analysis were emphasized with few questions asked about how this material would ultimately be utilized. But in the nations where we were creating constabularies, intelligence, such as it was, had traditionally been largely an instrument of internal political control and repression. When national forces took control intelligence quickly reverted to this pattern, only now it was notably more efficient.

14. Communications between those making policies in Washington and those assigned to carry them out in the field always cause problems. With modern communications, directives from Washington arrive with the speed of light, however responses from those in the field often seem to travel with the speed of an intoxicated turtle. The

turnover to national command in Nicaragua was a prime example. Those making policy persisted in the illusion that a nonpartisan force could somehow be maintained, while those dealing directly with the *Guardia Nacional* knew better. But experience had taught them that arguing such cases with higher authority accomplished nothing and could be career threatening. In such cases, simply continuing the form of policy without the substance becomes the rule, and keeping the lid on for the moment, the "not on my watch" syndrome becomes standard operating procedure. Being able to honestly assess situations during operations, rather than long after, would be a major step towards making security force creation and training a more effective element of national policy.

15. If there is a final principle, it is that an ability to learn from the past is always essential. Past experiences cannot be replicated. What works in one situation may not work at all in another context. The effort to apply examples from the Philippines to the Latin American nations well-illustrates this. We usually learn more from mistakes than from success. History rarely teaches us what will work, but it can demonstrate what doesn't and can put us on our guard against the inevitable tide of unintended consequences.[10]

At the end of his study of intervention, Richard N. Haass wrote:

> Getting it right will be difficult. Policymakers must always exercise judgment. Guidelines are just that; they are not rules, much less absolutes. Interests alone do not provide answers or dictate choices. One must begin with an assessment of whether intervention is desirable, then address its feasibility, and then return to the question of desirability. . . . Making policy is always about choosing, deciding whether to intervene with military force is no exception. It is only that the stakes are greater.[11]

This advice applies not only to the issue of intervening but to specific policies related to such a decision, notably the development of new security forces. We ignore the lessons of past experiences at our peril. This was summed up by my maternal grandfather who was fond of observing, "If our foresight was as good as our hindsight we'd be better off by a damn sight."

Notes

1. Andrew J. Bacevich, "The Realist Persuasion," *Boston Globe*, 6 November 2005, http://www.boston.com/news/globe/ideas/articles/2005/11/06/the_realist_persuasion.

2. In recent decades this has slowly begun to change in many nations. But this was the dominant pattern in the first half of the 20th century.

3. Much of what follows is taken from Richard L. Millett, "The Limits of Influence: Creating Security Forces in Latin America," *Joint Forces Quarterly*, No. 42 (3rd quarter, 2006), 14–16.

4. Commander J.D. Helm to *Jefe Director, Guardia Nacional*, 13 November 1930, "Annual Sanitary Report of the *Guardia Nacional de Nicaragua* for the Year Ending September 30, 1930," Records of the *Guardia Nacional de Nicaragua*, RG 127.

5. Robison to Welles, 11 August 1922, National Archives and Record Service, Records of the United States Department of State, RG 59, 839.1051/25.

6. Captain Herbert S. Kemmling to Major Fleming, 11 March 1933, National Archives and Record Service, Records of the United States Marine Corps, RG 127, Entry 198.

7. Numerous discussions I have had on this subject, including those with a former Haitian Minister of Justice, a senior US Commander in Afghanistan, and the first director of Panama's Public Force confirm this trend.

8. For a current, if somewhat exaggerated example of these problems, see Jeff Sharlet, "Jesus Killed Mohammed: The Crusade for a Christian Military," *Harper's Magazine* (May 2009), 31–43.

9. Author's discussions with an American linguist working in Haiti in 1998 and with a US educated Haitian in 2006.

10. For another view of what this period of our history can teach us, see John B. Judis, *The Folly of Empire: What George W. Bush Could Learn from Theodore Roosevelt and Woodrow Wilson* (New York, NY: Scribner, 2004).

11. Richard N. Haass, *Intervention: The Use of American Military Force in the Post-Cold War World* (Washington, DC: The Carnegie Endowment for International Peace, 1999), 56.

Bibliography

Government Documents and Primary Sources

College Park, MD and Washington, DC, National Archives and Record Service, General Records of the Navy Department, Record Group 80.

College Park, MD and Washington, DC, National Archives and Record Service, Naval Records Collection of the Office of Naval Records and Library, Record Group 45.

College Park, MD and Washington, DC, National Archives and Record Service, Records of the Isthmian Canal Commission, 1904–14 and the Panama Canal, 1914–51, Record Group 185.

College Park, MD and Washington, DC, National Archives and Record Service, Records of the Military Government of Santo Domingo, Record Group 38.

College Park, MD and Washington, DC, National Archives and Record Service, Records of the United States Department of State, Record Group 59.

College Park, MD and Washington, DC, National Archives and Record Service, Records of the United States Marine Corps, Record Group 127.

Columbus, Ohio, Ohio State Historical Archives, Papers of Warren G. Harding.

Hagerty, Richard A., ed. *Haiti: A Country Study*. Washington, DC: Government Printing Office, 1989.

Hyde Park, NY, Franklin D. Roosevelt Presidential Library, Naval Affairs, Papers of Franklin D. Roosevelt.

Memoria de la Administración del Presidente de la Republica de Cuba, Mayor General Mario G. Menocal, durante el periodo Comprendidio entre el 1 de Julio de 1915 y el 30 de Junio 1916. Havana, Cuba: Secretaria de la Presidencia, 1919.

Munro, Dana Gardner to Richard L. Millett. 14 February 1965. Personal files of Richard L. Millett, Marine, IL.

New Haven, CT, Yale University Library, Historical Manuscripts Division, Papers of Ambassador Arthur Bliss Lane.

Quantico, VA, Marine Corps Historical Archives, Research Center, Papers of J.C. Breckinridge.

Quantico, VA, Marine Corps Historical Archives, Research Center, Papers of John A. Lejeune.

Quantico, VA, Marine Corps Historical Archives, Research Center, Papers of Smedley Darlington Butler.

United States Adjutant-General's Office. *Correspondence Relating to the War with Spain Including the Insurrection in the Philippines and the China Relief expedition, May 15, 1898 to July 30, 1902*, Vol. I. Washington, DC: Government Printing Office, 1903.

United States Agency for International Development. *US Overseas Loans and Grants and Assistance from International Organizations: Obligations and Loan Authorizations, July 1, 1945–September 30, 1980*. Washington, DC: Government Printing Office, 1980.

United States Congress. Senate. Select Committee on Haiti and Santo Domingo. *Inquiry into Occupation and Administration of Haiti and Santo Domingo: Hearings Before a Select Committee on Haiti and Santo Domingo.* 67th Congress, 1st and 2d Session, 1922.

United States Department of State. *Papers Relating to the Foreign Relations of the United States.* Vols. for 1909–1934. Washington, DC: Government Printing Office, various years.

United States Department of State. *Papers Relating to the Foreign Affairs of the United States: The Lansing Papers (1914–1920),* Vols. I and II. Washington, DC: US Government Printing Office, 1940.

Washington, DC, Library of Congress, Manuscripts Division, Naval Historical Foundation Collection, Papers of Admiral David Foote Sellers.

Washington, DC, Library of Congress, Manuscripts Division, Naval Historical Foundation Collection, Papers of Admiral William B. Caperton.

Washington, DC, Records of the Bureau of Insular Affairs, 1868–1945, Record Group 350.

Books

Ameringer, Charles. *Don Pepe: A Political Biography of José Figueres of Costa Rica.* Albuquerque, NM: University of New Mexico Press, 1978.

Arellano, Jorge Eduardo. *La Paz American en Nicaragua, 1910–1932.* Managua, Nicaragua: Academia de Geografia y Historia de Nicaragua, 2004.

Balch, Emily G., ed. *Occupied Haiti: Being the Report of a Committee of Six Disinterested Americans, representing organizations exclusively American, who, having personally studied conditions in Haiti in 1926, favor the restoration of the Independence of the Negro Republic.* New York, NY: The Writers Publishing Company, 1927.

Blount, James H. *The American Occupation of the Philippines, 1898–1912.* New York, NY: G.P. Putnam's Sons, 1913.

Boecker, Paul, Brinkely, Alan, and Pérez, Andres. *Henry L. Stimson's American Policy in Nicaragua.* New York, NY: Markus Weiner Publishing Inc., 1992.

Boot, Max. *The Savage Wars of Peace: Small Wars and the Rise of American Power.* New York, NY: Basic Books, 2002.

Brooks, Charles Morris. *Guarding the Crossroads: Security and Defense of the Panama Canal.* Panama: P & P Group, 2003.

Buckley, Kevin. *Panama: The Whole Story.* New York, NY: Simon and Schuster, 1991.

Calder, Bruce J. *The Impact of Intervention: The Dominican Republic During the US Occupation of 1916–1924.* Austin, TX: University of Texas Press, 1984.

Calixte, D.P. *Haiti: Calvary of a Soldier.* New York, NY: Wendell, Malliet & Co., 1939.

Carillo, Justo. *Cuba 1933: estudiantes, yanquis y soldados.* Miami, FL: Instituto de Estudios Interamericanos, 1985.

134

Castillero Pimental, Ernesto. *Panamá y Los Estados Unidos.* Second edition. Panama City, Panama City, Panama: Editor Humanidad, 1964.

Challener, Richard D. *Admirals, Generals, and American Foreign Policy.* Princeton, NJ: Princeton University Press, 1973.

Conniff, Michael L. *Panama and the United States: The Forced Alliance.* Second edition. Athens, GA: The University of Georgia Press, 2001.

Crassweller, Robert D. *Trujillo: The Life and Times of a Caribbean Dictator.* New York, NY: MacMillan Co., 1966.

Cronon, E. David. *Josephus Daniels in Mexico.* Madison, WI: The University of Wisconsin Press, 1960.

Cuestas Gómez, Carlos. *Soldados Americanos en Chiriquí.* Panama City, Panama: n.p., 1991.

Diedrich, Bernard. *Somoza and the Legacy of U.S. Involvement in Central America.* New York, NY: E.P. Dutton, 1981.

Ferguson, James. *Papa Doc, Baby Doc: Haiti and the Duvaliers.* Oxford, UK: Basil Blackwell, 1987.

Fermoselle, Rafael. *The Evolution of the Cuban Military, 1492–1986.* Miami, FL: Ediciones Universal, 1987.

Fishel, John T. "The Institutional Reconversion of the Panamanian Defense Forces." In *Post-Invasion Panama: The Challenges of Democratization in the New World Order,* ed. by Orlando J. Pérez, 16–22. Lanham, MD: Lexington Books, 2000.

Forbes, W. Cameron. *The Philippine Islands.* Revised edition. Millwood, NY: Kraus Reprint Company, 1976.

Franck, Henry A. *Zone Policeman 88.* New York, NY: Arno Press and the New York Times, 1970.

Fuller, Stephen M. and Cosmas, Graham A. *Marines in the Dominican Republic, 1916–1924.* Washington, DC: History and Museums Division, Headquarters, US Marine Corps, 1974.

Gates, John Morgan. *Schoolbooks and Krags: The United States Army in the Philippines, 1898–1902.* Westport, CT: Greenwood Press, 1973.

Gleijeses, Piero. *Shattered Hope: The Guatemalan Revolution and the United States, 1944–1954.* Princeton, NJ: Princeton University Press, 1991.

Goldwert, Marvin. *The Constabulary in the Dominican Republic and Nicaragua: Progeny and Legacy of United States Intervention.* Gainesville, FL: University of Florida Press, 1962.

Guevara-Mann, Carlos. *Panamanian Militarism: A Historical Interpretation.* Athens, OH: Ohio University Press, 1996.

Guzmán, Luis Humberto. "Nicaragua's Armed Forces: An Assessment of their Political Power." In *Beyond Praetorianism: The Latin American Military in Transition,* ed. by Richard L. Millett and Michael Gold-Biss. Miami, FL: The North-South Center Press, University of Miami, 1996.

Haass, Richard N. *Intervention: The Use of American Military Power in the Post–Cold War World.* Washington, DC: The Carnegie Endowment for International Peace, 1994.

135

Hartlyn, Jonathan. *The Struggle for Democratic Politics in the Dominican Republic*. Chapel Hill, NC: The University of North Carolina Press, 1998.

Healy, David F. *Gunboat Diplomacy in the Wilson Era: The United States Navy in Haiti, 1915–1916*. Madison, WI: The University of Wisconsin Press, 1976.

_____. *The United States in Cuba, 1898–1902: Generals, Politicians, and the Search for Policy*. Madison, WI: The University of Wisconsin Press, 1963.

Heinl, Robert D. and Nancy G. *Written in Blood: The Story of the Haitian People, 1492–1971*. Boston, MA: Houghton Mifflin, 1978.

The International Institute for Strategic Studies. *The Military Balance, 1985–1986*. London, UK: The International Institute for Strategic Studies, 1984.

Jones, Howard. *The Bay of Pigs*. New York, NY: Oxford University Press, 2008.

Jorden, William J. *Panama Odyssey*. Austin, TX: University of Texas Press, 1984.

Judis, John B. *The Folly of Empire: What George W. Bush Could Learn from Theodore Roosevelt and Woodrow Wilson*. New York, NY: Scribner, 2004.

Kagan, Robert. *A Twilight Struggle: American Power and Nicaragua, 1977–1990*. New York, NY: The Free Press, 1996.

Karnow, Stanley. *America's Empire in the Philippines*. New York, NY: Random House, 1989.

Koster, R.M. and Sanchez, Guillermo. *In the Time of the Tyrants, Panama, 1968–1990*. New York, NY: W.W. Norton and Co., 1990.

Kretchik, Walter E., Baumann, Robert F., and Fishel, John T. *Invasion, Intervention, "Intervasion," A Concise History of the US Army in Operation Uphold Democracy*. Fort Leavenworth, KS: US Army Command and General Staff College Press, 1998.

Laguerre, Michael S. *The Military and Society in Haiti*. Knoxville, TN: The University of Tennessee Press, 1993.

Lake, Anthony. *Somoza Falling: The Nicaraguan Dilemma, A Portrait of Washington at Work*. Boston, MA: Houghton Mifflin, 1989.

Langley, Lester. *Banana Wars: An Inner History of American Empire, 1900–1934*. Lexington, KY: The University of Kentucky Press, 1983.

Leonard, Thomas M. *US Policy and Arms Limitation in Central America: The Washington Conference of 1923*. Los Angeles, CA: Center for the Study of Armament and Disarmament, California State University–Los Angeles, 1982.

Linn, Brian McAllister. *Guardians of Empire: The U.S. Army and the Pacific, 1902–1940*. Chapel Hill, NC: The University of North Carolina Press, 1997.

_____. *The Philippine War, 1899–1902*. Lawrence, KS: University of Kansas Press, 2000.

_____. "The US Army and Nation Building and Pacification in the Philippines, 1902–1940." In *Armed Diplomacy: Two Centuries of American Campaigning*. Fort Leavenworth KS: Combat Studies Institute Press, 2004.

Liss, Sheldon B. *The Canal: Aspects of United States–Panamanian Relations.* South Bend, IN: University of Notre Dame Press, 1967.

Lockmiller, David A. *Magoon in Cuba.* Chapel Hill, NC: The University of North Carolina Press, 1938.

Macaulay, Neill. *The Sandino Affair.* Chicago, IL: Quadrangle Books, 1967.

Major, John. *Prize Possession: The United States and the Panama Canal, 1903–1979.* Cambridge, UK: Cambridge University Press, 1993.

Martin, John Bartlow. *Overtaken by Events.* Garden City, NY: Doubleday, 1966.

McCain, William D. *The United States and the Republic of Panama.* New York, NY: Russell and Russell, 1965.

McCrocklin, James H., comp. *Garde D'Haiti, 1915–1934: Twenty Years of Organization and Training by the United States Marine Corps.* Annapolis, MD: United States Naval Institute, 1956.

McCullough, David. *The Path Between the Seas.* New York, NY: Simon and Schuster, 1977.

Miller, Stuart Creighton. *Benevolent Assimilation: The American Conquest of the Philippines, 1899–1903.* New Haven, CT: Yale University Press, 1982.

Millett, Allan R. *The General: Robert L. Bullard and Officership in the United States Army, 1881–1925.* Westport, CT: Greenwood, 1975.

_____. *The Politics of Intervention: The Military Occupation of Cuba, 1906–1909.* Columbus, OH: The Ohio State University Press, 1968.

_____. *Semper Fidelis: A History of the United States Marine Corps.* Second edition. New York, NY: The Free Press, 1992.

Millett, Richard L. *Guardians of the Dynasty: A History of the US Created Guardia Nacional de Nicaragua and the Somoza Family.* Maryknoll, NY: Orbis Books, 1977.

Millspaugh, Arthur C. *Haiti Under American Control.* Boston, MA: World Peace Foundation, 1931.

Munro, Dana Gardner. *Intervention and Dollar Diplomacy in the Caribbean, 1900–1921.* Santa Barbara, CA: Greenwood Press Reprint, 1980.

_____. *The United States and the Caribbean Republics, 1921–1933.* Princeton, NJ: Princeton University Press, 1974.

Nelson, William Javier. *Almost a Territory: America's Attempt to Annex the Dominican Republic.* Newark, DE: University of Delaware Press, 1990.

Ortega Saavedra, General Humberto. *El Epopeya de la Insurrección.* Managua, Nicaragua: LEA Grupo Editorial, 2004.

Pastor, Robert A. *Condemned to Repetition: The United States and Nicaragua.* Princeton, NJ: Princeton University Press, 1987.

Pérez Jr., Louis A. *Cuba Under the Platt Amendment, 1902–1934.* Pittsburgh, PA: University of Pittsburgh Press, 1986.

_____. *Intervention, Revolution and Politics in Cuba, 1913–1921,* Pittsburgh, PA: University of Pittsburgh Press, 1978.

Perkins, Dexter. *A History of the Monroe Doctrine.* Revised edition. Boston, MA: Little Brown & Co., 1955.

Pezullo, Lawrence and Pezullo, Ralph. *At the Fall of Somoza.* Pittsburgh, PA:

University of Pittsburgh Press, 1993.

Pippin, Larry L. *The Remon Era: An Analysis of a Decade of Events in Panama, 1947–1957*. Palo Alto, CA: Stanford University, Institute of Hispanic and Luso-Brazilian Studies, 1964.

Platt, Senator Orville H. to Edwin F. Atkins. "Senator Orville H. Platt on Relations with Cuba, May 1901," 11 June 1901. In *An Old Fashioned Senator: Orville H. Platt of Connecticut* by Louis Arthur Coolidge (New York, NY: G.P. Putnam's Sons, 1910), 314.

Ramsey III, Robert D. *Savage Wars of Peace: Case Studies of Pacification in the Philippines, 1900–1902*. The Long War Series Occasional Paper 24. Fort Leavenworth, KS: Combat Studies Institute Press, 2008.

Ropp, Steve C. "National Security." In *Panama, A Country Study*, ed. by Sandra W. Meditz, Dennis Hanrath and Dennis Michael Hanratty (Washington DC: US Government Printing Office, 1989).

_____. *Panamanian Politics: From Guarded Nation to National Guard*. New York, NY: Praeger, 1982.

Sacasa, Juan Bautista. *Comó y por qué caí del poder*. Third edition. Managua, Nicaragua: Vanguardia, 1988.

Sands, William Franklin. *Our Jungle Diplomacy*. Chapel Hill, NC: The University of North Carolina Press, 1944.

Schmidt, Hans. *The United States Occupation of Haiti, 1915–1934*. New Brunswick, NJ: Rutgers University Press, 1971.

Scranton, Margaret. *The Noriega Years: U.S.-Panamanian Relations, 1981–1990*. Boulder, CO: Lynne Reiner Publishers, 1991.

Smith, Julian C., et al. *A Review of the Organization and Operations of the Guardia Nacional de Nicaragua*. Washington, DC: US Marine Corps Headquarters, 1937.

Smith, Robert A. *What Happened in Cuba: A Documentary History*. New York, NY: Twayne Publishers, 1963.

Spector, Robert M. *W. Cameron Forbes and the Hoover Commission to Haiti (1930)*. Lanham, NY: University Press of America, 1985.

Stimson, Henry L. *American Policy in Nicaragua*. New York, NY: Charles Scribner's Sons, 1927.

Thomas, Hugh. *Cuba: The Pursuit of Freedom*. New York, NY: Harper and Row, 1971.

Thomas, Lowell. *Old Gimlet Eye: The Adventures of Smedley D. Butler as Told to Lowell Thomas*. New York, NY: Farrar and Reinhart, 1933.

Tijerino, Gustavo. *El Terremoto mas barbaro de la historia*. Vols. I and II. Leon, Nicaragua: Instituto Technico La Salle de Leon, 1973.

Vanderwood, Paul J. *Disorder and Progress: Bandits, Police, and Mexican Development*. Lincoln, NE: University of Nebraska Press, 1981.

Vega, Bernardo. *Trujillo y las Fuerzas Armadas Norteamericanos*. Santo Domingo, Dominican Republic: Fundacion Cultural Dominicana, 1992.

Venzon, Anne Cipriano, ed. *General Smedley Darlington Butler: The Letters of a Leatherneck, 1898–1931*. New York, NY: Praeger, 1992.

Walter, Knut. *The Regime of Anastasio Somoza, 1936–1956*. Chapel Hill, NC: The University of North Carolina Press, 1993.

Watson, Bruce W. and Tsouras, Peter G., eds. *Operation Just Cause*. Boulder, CO: Westview Press, 1991.

Weiner, Tim. *Legacy of Ashes: The History of the CIA*. New York, NY: Doubleday, 2007.

Welles, Sumner. *Naboth's Vineyard: The Dominican Republic, 1844–1924*. Vols I and II. New York, NY: Payson and Clarke Ltd., 1928.

White, John R. *Bullets and Bolos: Fifteen Years in the Philippine Islands Fighting Insurgents with the Philippine Constabulary*. New York, NY: The Century Company, 1928.

Wiarda, Howard. *Dictatorship and Development: The Methods of Control in Trujillo's Dominican Republic*. Gainesville, FL: University of Florida Press, 1968.

Williamson, Charles T. *The United States Naval Mission to Haiti, 1959–1965*. Annapolis, MD: Naval Institute Press, 1969.

Wilson, James Harrison. *Under the Old Flag: Recollections of Military Operations in the War for the Union, the Spanish War, the Boxer Rebellion, Etc.* Vols. I and II. New York, NY: D. Appleton & Co., 1912.

Wirkus, Faustin, and Taney, Dudley. *The White King of La Gonâve*. Garden City, NY: Doubleday, Doran and Co., 1931.

Wise, Colonel Frederic M. and Frost, Meigs O. *A Marine Tells It To You*. New York, NY: J.H. Sears and Co., 1929.

Wood, Bryce. *The Making of the Good Neighbor Policy*. New York, NY: Columbia University Press, 1961.

Worcester, Dean C. *The Philippines, Past and Present*. Vols I and II. Whitefish, MT: Kessinger Publishing Company, 2004.

Yates, Lawrence A. *Power Pack: US Intervention in the Dominican Republic, 1965–1966*. Fort Leavenworth, KS: Combat Studies Institute Press, 1988.

_____. *The U.S. Military Intervention in Panama: Origins, Planning and Crisis Management, June 1987–December 1989*. Washington, DC: Center for Military History, United States Army, 2008.

Dissertations and Theses

Barker, Michael Lynn. "American Indian Tribal Police: An Overview and A Case Study." Ph.D. dissertation, State University of New York–Albany, 1994.

Gaddy, Glen D. "MacArthur's Development of the Philippine Army and the Defense of the Islands, 1935–1942." M.A. thesis, Southern Illinois University–Edwardsville, 1974.

Grossman, Richard. "Hermanos de la Patria: Nationalism, Honor and Rebellion: Augusto Sandino and the Army in Defense of the National Sovereignty of Nicaragua." Ph.D. dissertation, The University of Chicago, 1996.

Hance, Harry Thomas. "Civil-Military Relations: The Organization and Control of the Constabulary Force of the Republic of Haiti, 1915–1934." M.A. thesis, The Ohio State University, 1965.

MacMichael, David Charles. "The United States and the Dominican Republic, 1871–1940: A Cycle in Caribbean Diplomacy." Ph.D. dissertation, University of Oregon, 1964.

Pérez, Orlando J. "Elites, Power, and Ideology: The Struggle for Democracy in Panama." Ph.D. dissertation, University of Pittsburgh, 1996.

Polk, Freddy L. "Building Armies for Democracy: US Attempts to Reform the Armed Forces of Cuba (1906–1909) and Nicaragua (1927–1933)." Master of Military Art and Science thesis, US Army Command and General Staff College, Fort Leavenworth, KS, 1987.

Soloman, Marvin A. "Law, Order and Justice in the Dominican Republic During the United States Military Government." M.A. thesis, Southern Illinois University–Edwardsville, 1969.

Swilling, Chris. "The High Price of Neglect: The 1964 Flag Riots in Panama." M.A. thesis, Southern Illinois University–Edwardsville, 1993.

Periodicals

Bacevich, Andrew J. "The Realist Persuasion." *Boston Globe*. 6 November 2005. http://www.boston.com/news/globe/ideas/articles/2005/11/06/the_realist_persuasion.

Baker Jr., George W. "The Wilson Administration and Panama, 1913–1921." *Journal of Inter-American Studies*, Vol. VIII, No. 2 (April 1966), 279–293.

Bimberg Jr., Edward. "Black Bandits of Haiti." *Leatherneck* (August 1941), 6–9.

Carlson, Captain Evans F. "The Guardia as a Police Force." *Leatherneck*, Vol. XV (October, 1932), 20 and 62.

Denig, Lieutenant Colonel Robert L. "Native Officer Corps, Guardia Nacional de Nicaragua." *Marine Corps Gazette*, Vol. XVII (November 1932), 75–77.

Farolan, Ramon J. "Reveille: Anecdotes from the life of a constable." *Philippine Daily Inquirer*, 22 June 2009, http://opinion.inquirer.net/inquireropinion/columns/view/20090622-211740/Anecdotes-from-the-life-of-a-constable.

Fellowes, Edward A. "Training Native Troops in Santo Domingo." *Marine Corps Gazette*, Vol. VIII, No. 4 (December 1923), 215–233.

Grieb, Kenneth G. "Warren G. Harding and the Dominican Republic: US Withdrawal, 1921–1933." *Journal of Inter-American Studies*, Vol. XI, No. 3 (July 1969), 425–440.

Hanneken, Major Herman H. "A Discussion of the Voluntario Troops in Nicaragua." *Marine Corps Gazette*, Vol. XXVI (November 1942), 247–266.

Millett, Allan R. "The Rise and Fall of the Cuban Rural Guard, 1898–1912." *The Americas*, Vol. 29, No. 2 (October 1972), 192–211.

Millett, Richard L. "Anastasio Somoza Garcia: A Brief History of Nicaragua's Enduring Dictator." *Revista/Review Interamericana*, Vol. VII, No. 3 (Fall 1977), 486–508.

_____. "The Limits of Influence: Creating Security Forces in Latin America." *Joint Forces Quarterly*, No. 42 (3rd Quarter, 2006), 14–16.

_____. "Looking Beyond Noriega." *Foreign Policy*, No. 71 (Summer 1988), 46–64.

Millett, Richard L. and Gaddy, G. Dale. "Administering the Protectorates: The US Occupation of Haiti and the Dominican Republic." *Revista/Review Interamericana*, Vol. VI, No. 3 (Fall 1976), 383–402.

Millett, Richard L. and Soloman, Marvin. "The Court Martial of Lieutenant Rafael L. Trujillo." *Revista/Review Interamericana*, Vol. II, No. 3 (Fall 1972), 396–404.

Ormsbee Jr., William H. "U.S. Army School of the Americas (USARSA): Profile of a Training Institution." *DISAM Journal*, Vol. 7, No. 2 (Winter, 1984), 7–10.

"Our Casualties in Other Wars." *New York Times*, 1 January 1918, 44.

Pomeroy, Earl S. "America's Colonial Office." *The Mississippi Valley Historical Review,* Vol. 30 (March 1944).

Reisinger, Colonel H.C. "La Palabra del Gringo: Leadership in the Nicaraguan National Guard." *United States Naval Institute Proceedings*, Vol. LXI (February 1935), 215–221.

Scranton, Margaret. "Consolidation and Imposition: Panama's 1992 Referendum." *Journal of Inter-American Studies and World Affairs*, Vol. 35, No. 3 (Fall 1993), 65–102.

Sharlett, Jeff. "Jesus Killed Mohammed: The Crusade for a Christian Military." *Harper's Magazine* (May 2009), 31–43.

Smith, Lieutenant Colonel Richard W. "Philippine Constabulary." *Military Review* (May 1968), 73–160.

Interviews

Smith, Lieutenant General Julian C., USMC (Retired). Interview by author. Arlington, VA, April 1966.

Internet Sources

Dumindin, Arnaldo. *Philippine-American War, 1899–1902*. Online. Available at http://www.freewebs.com/philippineamericanwar/thewarrages1899.htm, accessed December 2009.

Hoover, President Herbert. "State of the Union Message." 3 December 1929. Available at www.let.rug.ni/usa/P/hh31/speeches/hh_1929.htm, accessed December 2009.

Roosevelt, President Theodore. "State of the Union Address." 5 December 1905. Available at http://www.theodoreroosevelt.com, accessed December 2009.

About the Author

Dr. Richard L. Millett received his A.B. with honors from Harvard and his M.A. and Ph.D. from the University of New Mexico. He taught at Southern Illinois University from 1966 through 1999 as well as at the University of Miami, the Air War College, and several universities in Colombia in 2000 and 2001. He held the Oppenheimer Chair of Warfighting Strategy at the Marine Corps University.

Millett has published numerous works on Latin America, including *Colombia's Conflicts: The Spillover Effects of a Wider War* (2002), *Beyond Praetorianism: The Latin American Military in Transition* (1996), and *Searching for Panama* (1993). His articles have appeared in *Foreign Policy, The Wilson Quarterly, Joint Forces Quarterly, Journal of Inter-American Studies, Current History, The New Republic*, and numerous other journals. Millett has also written articles for the Washington Post, Miami Herald, Los Angeles Times, and other national newspapers.

Dr. Millett is Vice President and Director of the St. Louis Committee on Foreign Relations and a member of the Board of the American Committees on Foreign Relations. He is also a Board Member and past Vice President of the Inter-American Defense College Foundation.

GPO U.S. GOVERNMENT PRINTING OFFICE: 2010—652-786